"If you want to read a book with heart—written from true, emotional depth—this is the one."
—Cecil Murphey, author and co-author of more than 100 books,
including *Gifted Hands: The Ben Carson Story* and
the *New York Times* best-seller, *90 Minutes in Heaven*.

"Pain never touches just our bodies. From the dentist's drill to the surgeon's scalpel, pain and sickness stick their uninvited noses into our deep places. Cindy Scinto has lived long in valleys none of us hope to ever see and shares one pearl of great price that all of us need—hope. For all who suffer or who hold the hand of one suffering, this book can be strong stuff. But then, most good medicine is."
—Dave Swartz, author, *Dancing With Broken Bones, The Magnificent Obsession,*
and *Embracing God: Drawing Closer to the God Who Loves You*

"Cindy Scinto truly has the heart to write this book—not only her new physical heart, but her spiritual heart. This is evidenced throughout these pages as she takes you along on her journey through over fifty heart procedures, some bringing her close to death. She had questions, yes, and sometimes even anger and resentment at the seemingly unfairness of the turn her life has taken. Ultimately, however, the reader is drawn into her acceptance of God's will and the peace she experienced at every juncture. No matter what you're going through today, *A Heart Like Mine* will cause you to hunger for more of God's presence in your life."
—Donna Clark Goodrich, author, *Healing in God's Time,* and *A Step in the Write
Direction—the Complete How-to Book for Christian Writers*

"*A Heart Like Mine* has been a great inspiration to Pastor Bob in this last message series. We, as a body, would like to thank you for writing your book and for bringing your words here to Mt. Spokane Church."
—Mt. Spokane Church
Mead, Washington

"Impacting and filled with profound, scriptural insight and spiritual depth gained through years of severe testing, Cindy writes *A Heart Like Mine* for every person who has ever wondered about God's will and suffering. A thought-provoking read for the serious Christian!"
—Dr. Robert V. Smith, Senior Pastor, Mt. Spokane Church
Moody Bible College Instructor, Spokane, Washington Campus
Chaplain, Spokane, Washington Fire Department

"I really enjoyed reading and sharing this book. What power in the hope we have in Christ alone. Your story becomes His story for us to gently walk alongside and see, if only for a moment, what few others have known: His heart through yours."
—Kena
Phoenix, Arizona

"It is truly inspiring to read this book because Cindy has written from actual experience, not just theory or preaching, and you can feel her pain, understand her searching, and follow her journey of 'Why me, God?' to 'How can I use this to help others?' This book will help you understand our life trials and how to deal with them!"

—Becky
Liberty Lake, Washington

"I just finished this book yesterday and WOW. I laughed, I cried, I pondered, I examined my own walk with Christ. This book paints such a visual experience of the author's journey to understanding God's will. It is well written and an easy read, loaded with profound scripture, and yet her personality shines through. All I can say is thank you, Cindy, for sharing. I have given two copies away as gifts and kept one for me. Several people on my Christmas list will be getting this book."

—Laura
Mesa, Arizona

"I liked your book so much that I ordered three more for friends. We have two friends with serious illnesses. One just had both of her kidneys removed and the other may have terminal cancer. Amazon says they are sold out and don't have a source to get more. You should send them a bunch!"

—Dick
Hayden, Idaho

"Wow, you did a most excellent job of writing and sharing your spiritual and physical journey! I finished the book in one day—you have a story that needed to be told. God definitely gave you powerful words to express what you have learned about Him and getting through suffering. Your book blessed me and I know God has plans for it to bless many more people. Thank you for finding time and answering God's call to write the book."

—Carol
Bend, Oregon

"How wonderful that you could share with us from such very personal struggles. I have sent a book to two nieces who are struggling with cancer and have had great positive feedback from them. We have all been inspired by how the Lord is leading you as we all fight the same emotional feelings in our personal battles. Looking forward to your next book."

—Virginia
Spokane, Washington

A Heart Like Mine

A Heart Like Mine

Finding God's Will for Your Life

CINDY VALENTI-SCINTO

Published by: Pleasant Word (a division of WinePress Publishing), PO Box 428, Enumclaw, WA 98022. ...as a custom, the ultimate design, content, editorial accuracy, and views expressed or implied in this work are those of the author.
ADELPHOS BOOKS
For info: www.cindyscinto.com

Unless otherwise noted, all Scriptures are taken from the *Holy Bible, New International Version*®, *NIV*®. Copyright © 1973, 1978, 1984 by Biblica, Inc.™ Used by permission of Zondervan. All rights reserved worldwide.

Scripture quotations marked KJV are taken from the *King James Version* of the Bible.

Scripture references marked NASB are taken from the *New American Standard Bible*, © 1960, 1963, 1968, 1971, 1972, 1973, 1975, 1977 by The Lockman Foundation. Used by permission.

ISBN 13: 978-1-4141-1497-2
ISBN 10: 1-4141-1497-4
Library of Congress Catalog Card Number: 2009905204

This book is dedicated to my heart donor, Danielle—my "angel on earth." Although I never knew you face-to-face, I know your very essence. Each time your heart beats in my chest, I am reminded of the life you gave so I could live.

Greater love has no one than this, that he lay down his life for his friends.

—John 15:13

Contents

Acknowledgments

FIRST OF ALL, my husband, John, deserves the utmost recognition for his unwavering dedication to holding up the proclamation "in sickness and health" as he takes care of me day after day, never stopping once to complain. I would not be here without his love, faithful help, encouragement, wisdom, and support. I love you.

And my son, Jonathan: You had to persevere through entering your teen years worrying your mom might not be alive when you came home from school each day. Much was delayed or missed due to my constant illness. I love you for being a caring, loving son who always found a way to cheer me up. I never will forget the first time I was in the ICU and you had your dad read Psalm 86 to me. You thought I would like how it spoke of God fighting for us and helping the needy. You are the best son anyone could grow up with!

The doctors and staff my life depended on and still does—I never can find a way to properly thank you all: special thanks to Dr. Canaday for believing in me and never using the word *psychology,* Dr. Chilson, Dr. Icenogle. Dr. Sandler, Dr. Sestero, Dr. Carol Wysham, Dr. Danko Martincic, who believes in nurturing a transplanted heart, Sacred Heart Medical Center staff, the nurses on 6-South and 6-North, ICU nurses, Carole Fenkner from Blue Cross/Blue Shield, Dr. Stegmann, Dr. Boehmer, the staff at the cath lab in Sacred Heart—especially dear, sweet "Carol" and big, bad "Dave," the staff at Spokane Cardiovascular Services, the paramedics with American Medical Response, and the ER nurses at Sacred Heart Medical Center who were there to usher me back to earth!

My heartfelt thanks, admiration, and appreciation go to Donna Goodrich for her incredible proofreading skills as she edited the first edition. But more importantly, Donna, you are my friend, mentor, and a godly woman who has taught me much.

Pastor Bob Smith and Pastor Steve Williams: You each took this book and have spoken volumes of wisdom and knowledge through the teaching series. "And I will give you pastors according to mine heart, which shall feed you with knowledge and understanding" (Jer. 3:15 KJV).

In memory are my dad, Joseph Valenti, who always encouraged me to write, and my brother Charlie, who was there for me when I needed him.

Charlotte, Danielle's mom—you have provided the completion for this book. I love you.

Thank You, God, for allowing all these people to have a hand in my life. You, my Father in heaven, started this journey and You will bring it to completion, in Your time.

Foreword

WITH MORE THAN thirty years as senior pastor of a large church, and as many years serving as chaplain for the local fire department, I regularly encounter people faced with a variety of challenging situations. Few with whom I have dealt have been tested as dramatically and severely as Cindy Scinto and her family.

The impact of Cindy's story is not to be found only in the life and death struggle of her failing physical heart and related medical difficulties. The penetrating power of this book is revealed in the testimony of her spiritual discoveries. It is the development of a spiritual heart—a heart that by faith has learned to rest in a God who proves Himself real in the unexpected storms of everyday life.

> I praise you because I am fearfully and wonderfully made; your works are wonderful, I know that full well. My frame was not hidden from you when I was made in the secret place. When I was woven together in the depths of the earth, your eyes saw my unformed body. All the days ordained for me were written in your book before one of them came to be.
>
> —Ps. 139:14-16 NIV

The Hebrew word for "ordained" means to form, fashion, shape, or frame human activity. It is to plan or purpose a situation. It relates to something or someone being predetermined or formed according to a divine plan and purpose. Biblically, it is often used of potters who form their creations.

A Heart Like Mine is the experience of a young wife and mother as she learns to embrace her days as ordained by God. Cindy's unforeseen and seemingly never-ending physical trials have turned her world upside down. This is a thought provoking account of a journey in understanding God's will for our lives in the midst of extreme difficulties.

Through God's Word and prayer, Cindy has gleaned timeless truths about a God who can be trusted even when our own hearts prove to be broken and flawed. This is a revealing portrait of each of our lives to one extent or another. It is a compelling call to recognize the human heart as fatally spoiled by sin. This book challenges readers to seek remedy in Jesus Christ and the spiritual transplant He alone can provide.

Biblically sound and well researched, Cindy writes *A Heart Like Mine* for every person who has ever wondered why bad things happen to good people.

—Dr. Robert V. Smith
Senior Pastor, Mt. Spokane Church
Moody Bible College Instructor, Spokane, Washington Campus
Chaplain, Spokane, Washington Fire Department

A Note from the Author

"I AM SO out of control!" And I love the way that sounds. But don't misunderstand—I am in no way reckless, dangerous, self-destructive, crazy, or anything even close. I am simply so out of control of my life and circumstances that I live in an absolutely peaceful and joyful way.

The trials I have experienced the past seven years allow me to write this book from firsthand experience. The list you are about to read illustrates how much I suffered in a short period of time. So when I say I have been broken and depressed, crushed and bewildered, and that I know what suffering is, I speak the truth. But it also should help you understand, as you read this book, that giving God complete control of my life did not happen without a battle of my will.

Here is a list of the major heart-related medical procedures and surgeries I endured from September 2001 until this writing in 2009. It does not include the myriad of problems and issues with doctors, appointments, nurses, travel, insurance, and finances. (A glossary of the medical phrases below is on page 173.)

September 2001: First heart attack. Heart angioplasty, stent in main artery, clear left artery

October 2001: Brachytherapy and stent (two separate angioplasties in one day)

December 2001:   Heart angioplasty, diagonal artery stent

January 2002:   Heart angioplasty

February 2002:   Heart angioplasty, main and left artery

February 2002:   Open-heart surgery, double bypass, complications, two surgeries in one day, critical condition

July 2002:   Heart angioplasty

August 2002:   Traveled to New York City, heart angioplasty, main artery ballooned, two stents placed, two angioplasties in one week

September 2002:   Heart angioplasty

October 2002:   Heart angioplasty, four stents are 50 percent under-deployed, one is blocking the main artery

October 2002:   Heart angioplasty, rotablation, brachytherapy, anemic, blood transfusion

November 2002:   Attempted cardiac ablation, rescheduled for December

December 2002:   Ablation and pacemaker

January 2003:   Main artery 90 percent blocked, ballooned/rotablation

January 2003:   Traveled to San Diego, heart angioplasty

March 2003:   Heart angioplasty

April 2003:   Surgery, clean out scar tissue, re-cut sternum bone and put back together

June 2003:   Heart angioplasty to find 98 percent blockage in middle of main artery

June 2003:   Heart angioplasty to clear out blockage and another stent placed

July 2003:   ER visit—severe tachycardia

August 2003:   Heart angioplasty

October 2003:   Heart angioplasty

December 2003:   Surgery in Pennsylvania—mini thoracotomy to inject FGF-1 Growth Hormone, experimental surgery

February 2004:   Heart angioplasty, main artery 99 percent blocked

February 2004:	Heart angioplasty, rotablation and brachytherapy
March 2004:	Heart angioplasty
May 2004:	Heart angioplasty, partial occlusion of artery—no intervention
August 2004:	Heart angioplasty, artery 100 percent occluded—no intervention
September 2004:	Heart angioplasty, two blockages in main artery—two more stents
September 2004:	Heart angioplasty, two blockages in main artery—two more stents
October 2004:	Heart angioplasty
December 2004:	Heart angioplasty
April 2005:	ER, went into cardiac arrest two times, almost died (read about my experience with death in Chapter 1)
April 2005:	Heart angioplasty, pre-heart transplant
July 2005:	Heart transplant!
January 2006:	Cytomegalovirus (CMV) detected, only treatment is chemotherapy
February 2006:	CMV returns, back on chemotherapy
May 2006:	CMV returns, go on a stronger chemotherapy, in hospital four weeks
October 2006:	CMV returns, in hospital four weeks, then on chemotherapy at home for three months
November 2007:	Broken right leg and knee
December 2008:	Double abdominal hernia repair needed due to scarring from operations and a broken sternal wire

If you made it through this list, you can begin to understand why I titled this book *A Heart Like Mine*. But keep in mind, I am here to encourage you to see that God gives us all a portion of faith—enough to make it through the toughest of trials and to emerge triumphant.

—Cindy

Here are three anchor verses God gave me early on in my illness. Use these to steady yourself as you find God's will for your life:

Deal courageously, and the LORD shall be with the good.
—2 Chron. 19:11 KJV

Do not grieve, for the joy of the LORD is your strength.
—Neh. 8:10

Beware of turning to evil, which you seem to prefer to affliction.
—Job 36:21

Introduction

ON SEPTEMBER 11, 2001, my heart ached for the lives lost in New York City. After all, that was my home—the place where I grew up. A week later, my heart broke once again—emotionally and physically.

Unremitting pressure and pain in my chest sent me to my family doctor. After three appointments and two emergency room visits, I was admitted to the advanced cardiac care unit of the local hospital. As I sat on the edge of a sterile hospital bed, I questioned why they had admitted me for heart problems. There was nothing wrong with my heart. I stared pensively at the flyers on the bulletin board describing discharge instructions after open-heart surgery.

I had no idea looming blockages in two of my coronary arteries were threatening to take my life.

At forty years old, I never had thought of my heart. Life was grand. I confidently checked off *no* for all heart disease risk factors on the doctor's office intake form. My diet was healthy, my cholesterol levels were perfect, and my lifestyle was tailored to an athletic regimen.

I had developed diabetes as a child, but all my life I was diligent about taking care of my health. I visited my doctor once every six months, where he reiterated his assessment: "You are healthier than patients I see who are not diabetic."

When I applied for life insurance, I was given the normal monthly rate instead of the higher rate given to people with diabetes. My exam, only a few years before my first heart attack, proved me to be in outstanding health.

All this was lost when I was inducted into the world of chronic heart disease. A permanent relationship with emotional and physical pain and disability emerged from this encounter.

The first procedure left me with a metal stent in my main artery, holding it open against the pressure of further assault. This was the start of a contentious battle to regain the vibrant health of which I had been robbed. The path I was constrained to follow threatened to dismantle my faith and unravel my plans.

I often fought to divert God's will for my life and stray from His delineated design. Now I know I wouldn't change the past and I feel privileged to have walked His perfectly designed plan.

In his book, *Dancing With Broken Bones*, David Swartz explains, "For many of us, spiritual growth sometimes means going down a path we would much rather detour around."[1]

There is no ending until we meet a new beginning.

CHAPTER 1 ❦

In the Beginning

I HATE WATCHING everyone go by while I'm stuck in here. I want my life back. Angry thoughts spilled over, accentuating my already depressive mood as I stared out the living room window. Almost four years of heart attacks, surgeries, procedures, and endless medical treatments had left me disabled and despondent—sentenced to lie incapacitated on an overused couch. Joggers running past, women pushing strollers, and elderly couples taking leisurely walks reminded me of the cruel confinement heart disease had forced on me. I was angry at the world outside and the people who paraded past, living their lives uninterrupted.

Resentment caused me to hate people I didn't even know. *Look at them out there. Don't they know how lucky they are?*

Watching out the front window day after day was like being a specimen in the glass tank of a science lab. The multi-colored pills and capsules I took every few hours became nothing more than the doctor's attempt to find a way to prevent another heart attack. I was sure they prescribed many of them out of desperation. No one knew what to do anymore. Three cardiologists actually refused to treat me—they were too scared they would run out of options. The only choice left was to keep me drugged so I couldn't laugh at a good joke. Laughing would be too hard on my heart. It didn't stop me from trying.

When visitors came, I tried to cover up my foul mood, complaining about the deepening indent in the couch where I sat. Joking was a way to make things better. I didn't want people to worry about me. Even though I laughed with them, secretly I was afraid to die. Thinking how pitiful my life was, I sunk deeper into the hollowed out cushion.

One afternoon, I realized brooding wasn't doing me any good so I thought some lunch might lighten my pessimistic mood. With feeble efforts, I pushed up from the couch, leaning as if an earthquake were swaying the floor beneath me. I could feel the skin stretch on my badly swollen legs.

My steps were careful—I was afraid too much pressure would rip open my ankles. Getting to the kitchen, I found leftovers in the refrigerator from dinner the night before. The plate of food was unappetizing but I picked at it with my fork. It was hard to eat anything without gagging.

Each time I swallowed a miniscule forkful, I had to run to the bathroom and throw up. I gave up on keeping down food and put the plate in the sink.

"Why do I feel so bad? Why was today different?" I hoped the sick feeling would go away.

I pressed my fist into my chest, hoping to relieve the squeezing pressure, but the symptoms persisted and crushing pain traveled from my heart up into my neck. *Not another heart attack? Not another grueling ER visit?*

Going to the ER had become insanely mundane. Ominous blockages came often, making the threat of a heart attack seem routine. *Maybe I'll call someone for a ride.* I had a bad habit of *not* calling 911. One side of me hated the embarrassment of needing emergency help while the other side wanted to deny the critical situation. I knew I could die if I asked a friend to drive me the twenty-one miles to the hospital instead of calling for an ambulance, but I remained indignant.

I hated to think I was weak or sickly.

The palpitating heartbeats pounded up to my head as if I had run full speed and stopped abruptly. This turned my stubbornness into anxiety and fear. Panic swept through my body like the lingering burn of a honeybee's sting.

I grabbed the phone and dialed 911.

"What is your emergency?" the operator asked without any emotion.

"I think I'm having a heart attack."

Her voice was expressionless as she verified my address and told me the paramedics were on the way. An empty loneliness came over me. I wanted her to say more, to tell me it was going to be OK. Silence, dotted by the clicking of her keyboard, lingered through the telephone.

Feeling dejected, I hung up.

What do I do now? Sitting on a chair and waiting seemed nonsensical. *How will the paramedics get in? The front door is locked.*

My hands grabbed onto the walls to steady myself as I started toward the downstairs entryway. After a few steps, weak, wobbly knees gave out and I fell to the floor. It felt as if an elephant were sitting on me.

I crawled the rest of the way to the landing and slid down the steps until I was able to reach up for the doorknob. The lock released with a clicking sound.

My exhausted body slumped with relief and the walls of the foyer towered above me as I glanced up from a curled position. *Oh, God, please don't let me die.*

Moments later the door opened and two paramedics stepped in with their gear. Their arrival brought relief. I knew they were in charge of my failing life.

Strong arms lifted my flaccid body off the floor and sat me on the bottom step. I looked up into the paramedic's face and a gentle expression stared down at me as he hooked up his equipment, placing monitors on my chest. Shortly after he turned on the portable EKG machine, erratic beeping blared.

The paramedic's thoughtful looks quickly disappeared. He was unable to measure my blood pressure, and heartbeats sketched erratically across the EKG screen. A routine call quickly had turned into a race for life.

Two more EMTs rushed up to the house and I watched them lift a bright yellow gurney onto the outside stoop. After some commotion, they leaned me against the hard, plastic board. It was an awful, insecure feeling as they carried me out to the front yard, my body limp and unsteadied.

One of the paramedics started an IV in my arm. Hanging my hand over the edge of the gurney, I stroked the cool grass. It was good finally to be outside.

I hazily gazed up at the bright blue sky. *What is all this for? I only need a ride.* And if something was really wrong, what about all those neighbors walking and jogging down the street? Where were they now that something terrible was about to happen? It felt like dying was an imminent reality and I wanted someone to be there, someone who could recount what happened to me that sunshiny day in April.

Soon it was quiet and all I heard was the distant traffic from the main road. Paramedics hurried around like voiceless workers, wrapping up things for the ride to the hospital. Three of them lifted the gurney onto a stretcher and after I was hoisted into the ambulance, loud barking broke the awkward silence as my dog, Jackson, bolted out of the house. He was my hero—my constant companion during the dreary days. I worried he might be lost outside after we left.

Jackson ran for the vehicle, jumped in, and planted himself next to me. His presence made the cold, antiseptic ambulance affable. I wanted him to stay with me, to curl up next to me so I wouldn't be alone. But I knew he had to get out.

Backed against the ambulance wall, he was intent on protecting me and he growled at the attempts to remove him, snarling and biting at the paramedics. I could hear the deep rumble in his throat, fair warning before his teeth snapped at each hand trying to reach him.

"We can't get him out!" one of them frantically complained.

"Tell him to chase the cat and he'll run into the backyard," I offered weakly to the paramedic in the ambulance. *Oh, please don't leave him behind, all alone.*

Finally, one of the EMT put on thick gloves, reached in, and gently grabbed him. He took Jackson into the house, quickly closing the front door after him. I could see Jackson staring dejectedly out the window as the ambulance's back doors were slammed shut. The sunshine disappeared and darkness fell on me as we pulled out of the driveway.

In the Beginning

The ambulance driver took off abruptly and the continuous rumble of road noise droned loudly. I couldn't hear anything else. The EMT continued to check my blood pressure and monitor my heart rate. He had no expression and said nothing to reassure me. I looked into his face and hoped he would smile or offer some comforting words. Nothing.

The stretcher was thin and hard and I wondered why it was made to be so uncomfortable. I tried to lay my hands across my stomach but I was too weak to keep my arms from sliding down. I feebly reached across and locked my fingers together to keep them from hanging. I felt as if I were lying on the wing of an airplane and the unsteadiness was about to toss me into a free fall.

Every time I thought I would vomit, dry heaves wrenched me into spasms and my hands would slip, sending my arms down to flagellate like the robot when he warned of danger on *Lost in Space*. I wanted the ride to come to an end.

The ambulance finally came to an abrupt halt at the hospital, where we were met by waiting ER personnel. Doors opened and for a moment I felt the warmth of sun on my face, only to be robbed of its brilliance by fluorescent lights in the emergency room hallway.

I looked up at the plasterboard ceiling tiles racing past as I quickly was wheeled into an examination room. Nurses and doctors ran in and within seconds I was being hooked up to a myriad of machines and monitors.

A nasal cannula was placed on my nose and the nurse turned on the oxygen. I hated the whiff of plastic burning through my nostrils with the gushing of air. It would be nice if you could pick a scent—anything besides that acrid, artificial smell.

Once all the machines were hooked up, beeping and high-pitched alarms sounded like an out-of-tune marching band. My heart beat furiously and sent a wave of sharp pain into my neck and right arm. Although I was still conscious, I felt like I was slipping away. I didn't know if it was the medicines being pushed through IV lines or the overwhelming nausea that was paralyzing me.

Slowly, the room became a blur. Screaming sounds from machines and panicky voices from personnel faded. The muted scene became as if I were watching through an old glass pane, wavy and rippled with age

Nurses and doctors raced to work on me.

"She's coding!" one nurse yelled. "She's not breathing and we don't have a pulse!"

Her alarmed look flashed briefly before me.

Although my lifeless body was being assaulted by attempts to start my heart back up, I wasn't concerned. I was still, placid and unable to do anything. It was like I was outside my body, looking down. Even though a steady calmness held me from fear, one thing was sure to me: I knew I was dying.

Watching from above the exam table was like hovering over a movie set as the actors played out a scripted scene. I was there, but in a mystical way I never had felt before. Because I was weightless and inert, none of the treatments being done had any effect on me. I felt no pain. I felt no fear.

Behind me was a powerful presence of pure white; not simply a bright light, but a pureness beyond feeble words found in any language. I was drawn to this backdrop, wanting to hold onto the motionless entity. It was omnipotent. I knew I was in God's presence. He was right there behind me, watching as if we were both producers monitoring the actor's parts.

I spoke to Him, inaudibly to anyone in the room or me. My thoughts were sufficient for both of us to communicate.

"Lord, please don't let me die here in this ER all alone. Please, Lord, save me."

Somehow, He assured me it wasn't time for me to go.

I took a gasp of air and regained consciousness. Harsh sensations of the real world smacked me out of the tranquil visitation. My body wriggled, and I felt my arms twist and contort. Cardiac seizures further threatened to take my life.

Alongside the exam table were doctors, nurses, and the hospital chaplain. *Something bad must have happened for the chaplain to be standing there with his white collar and prayer stole.*

"We thought we were going to lose you, young lady," one of the nurses chimed at me. She continued to pump medications through the IV lines.

Two doctors worked to calm the seizures and recover a stable heart rate so there would be no more near-death experiences. No one wanted to come that close again.

After I regained my senses, I watched the room buzz with activity as I lay on the table, helpless and wondering what all the fuss was about. I glanced up at the clock on the wall. *Jonathan will be wondering where I am.* I was supposed to pick up my son from school that afternoon. *I hope he is OK.*

Oh, no, John will be frantic when he gets the news. My husband was on a flight out of town for work. He would have to turn around and come home. All my thoughts were focused on getting out of that ER so I could pick up my son and get in touch with my husband.

"Can someone hand me my phone?" I asked. "I have to get a ride for my son."

"Listen, little lady," the nurse said, "you just concentrate on staying alive. We'll take care of any phone calls to your family." She pumped more medicine through the IV and I drifted off to a sedated state.

A near-death experience and an encounter with God changed my perspective about dying. I always feared how it could happen. Would I drown or suffer a painful, slow death? This phobia made me feel cowardly as a Christian. *Shouldn't I know that God is not going to let me die in a tortuous, painful way?* Grabbing on to a concept of total security in the face of death is something I never imagined I could do.

But those few moments I visited with God were unexplainable. I was at peace and felt protected when I transitioned to that altered state. In a way, I wanted to linger and remain where it was safe and repose. Even though I returned to the brutal reality of mortal life, the realization that death had no power over me freed me up to shrug off the dread of tragedy.

I spent a week in the hospital after my near-death extravaganza. Visitors entering my room were greeted by jokes about death and dying. It was entertaining for me and calming for them. A morbid sense of humor is easy to acquire once you spend as much time as I did on the advanced cardiac care unit.

That week, John, or Guido as I fondly thought of him, came to visit. He worked with my husband and earned his name for the brazen, true-to-life Italian ways he projected. Guido was from Chicago and he sported an attitude of confidence and indestructible defiance.

But when he showed up at my hospital room, he hesitated to step in the door. The gruff man, wearing an expensive Tessori suit, tiptoed in and approached my bed as if he were paying respects at a family funeral.

"Come on in," I coaxed him. "Look at me—I'm alive and breathing!"

"Oh, my God, look at you. I didn't know if you were dead or not." He grabbed a chair and sat. We laughed and joked until he was convinced I was OK.

"Take it easy, will ya?" he commanded on the way out.

My cardiologist also came in that afternoon and found me complaining about going home. "You are really in good spirits for someone who just went through what you did. But you aren't going home until we are sure this won't happen again." His inquisitive look begged the same question everyone was asking, "Where does your playful and carefree disposition come from?"

People filtered in and out of my room all day. It was rare to have a moment alone or any guarantee of privacy. Even at night the door flung open for every little event: check my vitals, inspect the IV lines, "Do you need anything?"

If I had needed anything, I would have called.

That first night, my mind raced with scattered thoughts about what had been a harrowing event. And I fussed over the inquisition I had received from many people: How did I keep such a good attitude?

I thought back to preparing for a test in school. The milky white paper is placed face down on the desk in front of me. I wiggle in the attached stationary chair, cold and hard, like a seat on a city bus.

When the command to begin is given, I quickly turn the paper over, questions staring up at me like empty expectations. If I had studied and knew the material, the answers came easily. Breezing through to the end, I would be confident in a good grade.

But if I hadn't studied, the questions were more like bulleted daggers, each one a hurdle to get past. Stumbling blindly through to the end, I would anticipate the failing grade, noted in permanent red ink.

For any test, being intimate with a subject allows the skill needed to succeed. King Solomon says it well: "If the ax is dull and its edge unsharpened, more strength is needed but skill will bring success" (Eccl. 10:10).

I found myself close to death so many times that if I hadn't prepared my heart and wasn't able to perceive my strength in God, I would not have lived through all I did.

Wednesday, July 13, 2005, the heart surgeon sauntered into my hospital room. He had a flat way of handing out the worst news. I hated his blunt packaging but appreciated how he left no question unanswered. With the impassive manner you might see from a car mechanic listing mundane repairs needed for your vehicle, he delivered his assessment.

"We won't be able to get you a donor heart for nine months to a year," he told me, "and you don't have a year. We will keep you here on medications so you will be comfortable."

Comfortable? How grim is that?

There were some options to make it safer for patients waiting for a donor heart. Ventricular Assist Devices (VAD) can be used as a "bridge" to a heart transplant. Machinery is surgically woven into your abdomen, and tubes and wires connect to your heart to help it keep up with your body's demands. But that surgery would be too dangerous for me.

He left my room as gauntly as he had come in.

The next morning, I woke up at 6:30 A.M., contorted between flimsy, bleached hospital sheets and IV tubing. Unwinding my way out of bed, I grabbed my IV pole and headed for the sink.

My reflection in the mirror was a sight: scary, frazzled hair; sunken eyes; pale cheeks; and blue lips. I had been reduced to living as a corpse on life support and had no expectation of good news. It was an unhoped for possibility—a donor heart becoming available before my fight to live caved from the feeble resources left in my own heart.

I reached for my toothbrush and saw that a note had been insidiously placed on the sink. "NPO" was printed in large, black letters on fluorescent lime-green paper.

NPO was short for "nothing by mouth" and was meant to warn the nurses not to let me eat or drink anything. The dreaded instruction usually preceded a test or surgery. It was of no concern to me to be deprived of food or drink because I had no appetite, especially for hospital food.

My thoughts imagined, for a moment, there might be a donor heart for me. I fought the urge to get excited and hopeful. Disappointment was too familiar. I hated the anticipation of a life-saving opportunity being squashed by a false alarm.

Nurses traversed in and out of my room, rummaging through the medication draw, checking tubing, vitals, and my EKG. They were silent, but I could read their faces. I even imagined they were smiling—secretly.

He got a heart for me; I know he did.

At 8:30, the heart surgeon entered my room, stoic as always.

"Sign on the dotted line," he said as he placed a consent form in front of me.

I saw the words *Heart Transplant* written on the permission line, but I had to ask.

"What for?"

"You want a new heart, don't you?" His matter-of-fact mannerism made me wonder if this was a cruel joke. But it couldn't be. He never joked.

"How did you find a donor?" The words left my mouth and I cringed with the freaky feeling of a conversation based on someone's untimely death.

"A twenty-eight-year-old woman died near Seattle. She's an organ donor, but the transplant centers in the Northwest region turned down her heart for donation. There was too much damage."

"What makes you think this heart will work for me if all the other transplant centers turned it down?"

"Because this is the one the Lord has for you." There was composed confidence in his reply.

Looking at his intent expression, I answered without hesitating.
"I totally trust you."

No heart surgeon takes a transplant surgery lightly. Transplanting a damaged heart is rarely done. Both of us knew the situation was desperate.

As soon as my pen came up from the paper, he grabbed the permission forms and hurried out the door.

Nurses and technicians rushed into my room. It was an army of inquisitions and preparations for the ultimate surgery. Each one had a particular assignment, and they worked like trained paratroopers with specific coordinates.

John was a few miles away at work. I called him before the commotion got out of control, nervously punching the numbers on my cell phone. When he picked up I blurted the news before he could speak.

"John, he got a heart for me. Come over here now."

"I'll be right there."

He arrived in minutes, entering the room quietly and sidestepping the entourage.

I laid helpless while nurses flipped me from side to side, checking IV sites, adding more bottles of dripping medicines, and lathering my skin with brown, soupy betadine. I was the tin man from *The Wizard of Oz* being prepped for my wish to come true: "I could stay young and chipper and I'd lock it with a zipper, if I only had a heart."[2]

John leaned against the window, watching in astonishment. Deep whirring sounds from the MedStar helicopter leaving the hospital roof cut through the chatter and noise. We both looked out the large, gleaming window as the black and yellow chopper careened into the blue sky. Inside were the heart surgeon, surgical equipment, and his own surgical team. They were whisked off to a small, gravel-lined airport where a Lear jet was waiting on the runway to fly them over to Seattle. Time was not a luxury.

Once preparations were completed, I was transported down to the OR waiting room. The mundane ride through the hallways was peppered with smiling congratulations as familiar faces cheered me on. I glanced at them from my stretcher. Word was out that a donor heart was being acquired. This was breaking news to the many "captives" doing time in their own prisons. Pole pushers, those who shuffled the halls toting IV poles, peered out at the commotion. Pangs of guilt co-mingled with feelings of relief as I anticipated life on the other side.

The blue curtained cubicle in pre-op, illuminated with artificial fluorescent lights, faced the doors to the OR. John stood next to me as the transplant coordinator fired off scattered instructions on what to expect.

"If the doctor decides the heart cannot be repaired, you may wake up to find out nothing was done." Her mannerism was callous and dictated as she rambled on about possible disappointments. Tightness and pain radiated across my chest, signaling impending doom. The familiar threat lunged me into a panic.

I interrupted her rambling. "The chest pain is getting bad."

Immediately, an anesthesiologist began the medications to place me in a deep sleep of unawareness.

I looked up at John's concerned face.

"When I wake up next and see you, I will say 'I made it!'" My eyes succumbed to the anesthesia.

Ten hours later I woke up in intensive care momentarily. Through an oxygen mask and with dry, cracked lips, I whispered the words to John.

"I made it!"

For the next twelve hours, I would lie there in the cardiac intensive care unit, unaware of the significant event that had transpired. My heart surgeon, Dr. Icenogle, had arrived in Seattle with his team to find my donor's heart needed extensive work. Weeks after the surgery, I would learn he did more repairs on this heart than any other heart that had been transplanted from an unacceptable donor.[3]

The idea of someone dying tragically and unexpectedly is baffling. The actuality that their heart now beats in my chest is beyond comprehension. Adding to it the trauma of receiving a repaired heart is like announcing your life has been spared but the replacement parts may not be reliable.

But I am alive. I know this was the right donor heart for me. It was as if it were meant to be a part of me. The operating report stated that without all the techniques needed to get a transplanted heart to start pumping, this heart began beating as soon as it was placed in my chest and my own blood began to flow through it.

My own blood is pumping through someone else's heart. The assurance from the doctors was, "You will be exchanging one set of problems for another—but you will be alive." The promise of being alive was fulfilled. The promise of a new set of problems had only begun.

The week I spent in the cardiac intensive care unit after my transplant surgery was blanketed by the dark, eerie environment of the segregated rooms. When I awoke to a communicative state, I glanced out at the sterilization corridor to my room where a nurse was suiting up to come in and check on me. She peered out from blue, wrinkled garb covering all but her thin face.

"Hey, you in there, stop thrashing around!" Her demanding tone sparked me to rise out of the semi-conscious state holding me at bay.

"Hey, you out there, stop yelling at me!" I was equally testy.

"Well, you are quite the feisty one." She entered my sanitized room and got busy, checking all the connections and wires. My first impression of her left me defensive, but during my stay in that depressing unit she would become my best ally, and I looked forward to her shifts.

My goal was evident: do what I had to so I could be moved to the advanced cardiac care unit up on the sixth floor. At least there were windows there. CICU was situated under the ground floor. Darkness invaded every corner. Time stopped and days ran into each other like one continuous existence. Except for shift changes, I had no sense of time or what day of the week it was.

Advances toward freedom came in tiny achievements. Sitting in a chair defied gravity as my beaten body slumped over from its own weight. Cold plastic nipped my legs with a cooling sensation, a welcome change from the tepid sheets of the bed. My movements were calculated; I didn't want to jeopardize the progress.

In a solemn moment, when reprieve came from the multitudinous, non-stop care, I looked around the room, my container, and tried to fathom an event that felt so hollow.

Why don't I feel more enamored that my life has been saved? Why are my actions mundane? Incarceration in CICU was like a stretch of obscure emptiness necessary to reboot my life, like a plane taxiing on the runway before taking off for a new destination.

It would be a long time before I understood the concept of someone else's heart beating in my chest.

The week dragged on and levels of improvement reached the goal for freedom from my abyss. When I saw the arrival of a wheelchair driven by a familiar transport employee, his smile beckoning me, I felt like my life was ready to begin. Sitting in the vehicle to carry me out of limbo-like confinement, I glanced at the shut doors of other unfortunate inhabitants, my newly transplanted heart sinking for their fate.

Arrival on six south was triumphant. Rooms I begrudged many times before now promised light and life. Asking to be allowed to sit by the window, I basked in the warm summer sun penetrating the thick glass. One more week of scrutinizing medical care and education would buy me a ticket home.

I never want to find myself in the depths of cardiac intensive care again. Whenever I ride the elevator in the hospital, the lighted button for the second floor glares with creepy defiance. "That's one floor nobody should have to be admitted to," I warn.

Before my heart transplant, I was an inpatient fifty-four times in five years. I occupied the same rooms more than once on the advanced cardiac care unit. The hotel-like décor, plain, thin, and failing, was as deficient as the condition of each room's inhabitants.

Many times I glanced up at the pale green walls and gazed angrily at the flyers posted on the bulletin board. Their colored pages stared defiantly at me: "Open Heart Surgery Class," "Heart Healthy Nutrition Class," "Home Care for Bypass Patients," "Cardiac Rehabilitation." I was a prisoner to their defiance, a prisoner to the myriad of bottles dripping fluids into my veins, and a prisoner to the fear that consumed me.

The first procedure, in September 2001, swooped down on me with the swiftness of a predator hawk. Being admitted to the hospital for heart disease was incomprehensible.

Three weeks before, canoeing with friends, I had been unstoppable.

The Coeur d'Alene River meandered out from the boat launch, motionless and tranquil. It was late August. Water levels were low but our group of eager paddlers launched out to canoe the winding river deep into its uncultivated realm.

Sun warmed our backs, instigating frequent stops to dive into the crisp, cool water. Occasional water fights kept rowers busy dodging those with larger soaker guns randomly aimed at each other. My techniques for retaliation were ferocious, causing our canoe to careen wildly, water lapping up the sides.

"Mom, you're doing it again," complained my son, Jonathan, frantically grabbing the sides of the boat.

Unmoved by his desperate plea, I continued erratic techniques to avoid being attacked. A blissful day quickly turned into a race to the end where relay vehicles sat at the last boat ramp. Defeat was not part of my plan.

In defiance, I sang out, "So I'd like to know where you got the notion. Said I'd like to know where you got the notion to rock the boat. Don't rock the boat, baby. Rock the boat. Don't tip the boat over. Rock the boat. Don't rock the boat, baby. Rock the boat."[4]

Jonathan requested to switch canoes.

Propelled with intense fervor, I made my goal, reaching the end first. Using Herculean strength fed by victory, I dragged our canoe up the cement ramp single-handedly.

But the triumph of reaching the end of my trek soon would be shadowed by an onslaught of anguish as heart failure symptoms crept in over the following weeks.

I walked along the creek, glancing at my watch and quickening my pace. The pedometer strapped to my arm read seven-tenths of a mile. Warm moisture laid on my skin like condensation on a cold glass of iced tea on a hot summer day.

I began to gasp for air while my heart skipped beats, feeling as if there were butterflies fluttering in my chest. Sharp pain jolted across to my right arm. I slowed down and followed the winding blacktop path, calculating how long it would take me to get home.

My sweat-soaked T-shirt created a cool sensation as the slight breeze weaved between its folds. The path ended at a steep embankment littered with gravel and small rocks. Slippery steps led me to the street above and I picked up the pace, heading to my house.

Inside, I kicked off my sneakers and plopped on the couch. My heart had slowed its maddening pulse but the pain across my chest persisted.

For two days the same routine continued until I reluctantly went to see my family doctor. Blood work, EKG, blood pressure—everything was normal. I went home and took it easy, as the nurse had instructed.

After off-and-on sleep, I woke the next morning to the same issues nagging at me with a persistent presence. I called the doctor's office. This time they had me come in immediately and report upstairs to an unfamiliar room.

I opened the door to the stale smell of antiseptics and aged wood paneling. Instead of taking the elevator, I walked up to the second floor. *I can take the stairs. I'm not like the people in the waiting room. I'm healthy.*

I reached the top of the steps and grabbed the cold metal banister, straining to breathe. When I saw the technician come out of the exam room, I straightened and smiled.

"Come on in. We're going to take a look at your heart using an echocardiogram."

I climbed up on the papered table, dangling my legs over the edge like a kid waiting for instructions to open wide and say, "Ah."

"Lay back, please. This will take about forty-five minutes." The technician fired up the equipment and lathered a transducer with gel to help sound waves bounce off my heart, sending pictures back to the video screen. She pressed the plastic probe to my chest, sliding it across my skin. The icy cold sensation startled me but my attention quickly focused on the black and gray video screen as it came to life with images of my beating heart.

Watching the spectral shades of muscle and tissue rhythmically pace on the monitor lurched me into thoughts of early mortality. I felt something was wrong even though I had no idea what I was looking at. The technician worked silently.

After the echocardiogram was finished, I marched back down the steps to the main office, where I took a seat among the waiting. I kept my eyes from making contact so I wouldn't have to talk to anyone. This was not my club and I didn't want anyone to think I belonged.

The nurse called me in to see the doctor. Baffled by my complaints, he told me the results showed my heart was fine. "Here's a prescription for nitroglycerin tablets. When you have the chest pain, place one under your tongue and let it melt. That should help."

I shoved the paperwork in my purse and left, feeling stupid at even being there. The doctor mentioned it may be hormonal or anxiety.

"Are you worried or stressed?" he had asked me.

Maybe it was acid reflux. "Do you have frequent heartburn?" he had inquired.

I wasn't stressed, had no reason to have hormonal problems, and never got heartburn. *Fine, I'll go home and forget it.*

Later that night, after dinner, I couldn't set it aside.

"John," I bugged my husband, "please take me to the pharmacy to get this prescription filled. I have to try it and see if it helps."

We handed the pharmacist the prescription. It was late. A long line of tired people waited at the pick-up window, faces watching forward for a chance to move up closer. I leaned on the wall, letting John take a spot with the others. Pain shot up through my chest, boiling over with tightness and grabbing my neck. I walked to the front of the line and stepped up to the counter.

"If you don't give me that nitro now, I'll have a heart attack right here in the store." No one questioned my intrusion.

The pharmacist quickly handed me a small, brown glass bottle. While John paid, I opened it and placed the tiny white tablet under my tongue. Within seconds, a rush of cool relief flooded my chest. But by the time John was done paying, the pain and pressure were back.

"I guess if this helped even for a few minutes," I said, "something must be wrong. We need to go to the ER."

We walked out to the car and the cool night air made it easier to breathe. John drove to the hospital two miles away. I feebly explained to the intake nurse how the nitro had helped but only for a few minutes. While John filled out paperwork, I was taken in a wheelchair to a room and examined by a doctor. His disheveled white coat and messy hair framed the concern on his face.

"We have to get you to the hospital downtown so they can do further testing." I watched him rush out as soon as he uttered the words, leaving me sitting there with no idea of what was happening.

"Do you want to go by ambulance?" a nurse asked numbly.

"No, can my husband drive me?" No one had told me anything was wrong. *I don't need an ambulance unless it's serious.*

We got to the hospital downtown. By this time it was 1:30 A.M. and the waiting room was packed with sick people. Coughing, moaning, crying, and mumbled conversations made a symphonic backdrop of sound against the staff's orderly instructions.

Once I was back in the ER triage area, plans were made for me to perform an exercise stress test so heart problems could be ruled out. By the time I got wired up and was made to walk on a treadmill, it was five A.M.

The results came by way of another new doctor. Each time someone gave me more bad news, it was as blatant as the one before. I was on an assembly line of information and each phase brought me closer to a final piece of the puzzle. Blankly, he stated the prognosis. A heart catheterization had to be done to find and repair a suspected blocked artery that was robbing my heart of blood flow.

Early that afternoon, after endless paperwork and consent forms, I waited in a hospital room, watching the second hand on the wall clock tick away time. I didn't notice the sunny day outside. John was sitting next to my bed, his face pale and worn.

"I have one request." I spoke softly to him. "You have to promise me you will not be angry with God if He takes me today."

He turned away without answering.

"Look at me and promise." I insisted this time.

John turned, his face revealing the pain. How could I expect him to answer? I was OK with that and settled my head back into the pillows.

Moments later, transport personnel arrived. Their entrance to my room stirred up activity and broke the heavy silence. John followed as they wheeled me to the patient elevators and down to the heart catheterization lab.

Before I entered the final doors to the lab, John leaned over and caressed my forehead. Praying softly for the procedure to go well, he kissed my cheek.

In the OR, calming, sedative medications flowed through the IV line. They rendered me semi-awake but conscious enough to understand what was happening.

Two doctors, faces masked from recognition, worked to find and clear the blockage detected during earlier testing.

I watched from my drugged state as they compared monitors displaying my beating heart.

A few days earlier, in my doctor's office, I had been stunned by the images on the screen as the technician scanned my chest with an ultrasound machine. The shadowy, beating object looked nothing like I had expected, its ominous appearance lifting banefully to a rhythmic beat.

Here I was again, watching the screen and glancing anxiously, fearing my heart's next expansion would be its last as it pulsed much needed blood through my veins.

After some commotion, another doctor, his face contorted with deep concern, entered the operating room and mumbled directions to the surgical assistants. If the blockages could not be cleared, open-heart surgery was the next option.

Their conversations were difficult to follow, but the hurried activity told me things were worse than expected.

After watching several painstaking attempts, the blockages finally were cleared. Weaving the catheter tube through the blocked artery, the doctor used a balloon to enlarge the artery and then placed a stent (a woven metallic tube) to keep it open.

"They're done." A nurse leaned over and reassured me that the procedure was successful. "We'll let your husband know. He can see you in recovery."

Later that day I had a visit from my cardiologist. His relief was evident.

"If you had suffered a heart attack, it would have been fatal. The blockages were extensive. We refer to them as widow makers—they are more common in men and usually strike with no symptoms, killing instantly."

I struggled to understand what had happened to me. Blocked arteries had loomed in the hazy balance of keeping the blood flow sufficient to supply my heart muscle with much needed blood and oxygen. Within minutes, I could have been gone.

A senseless disruption on my life left me with questions. *Is this over now? Can I go on with my life? What happens next?*

After being properly educated and instructed in after-care for a heart procedure, I was discharged and left the hospital with my mind clamoring to understand the strike against my life. I was violated. *This will never happen again.*

But it did. Three years after the first blockages impaired my heart, I boasted of thirty-six visits to the catheterization lab.

One day I walked down the familiar hallway to the records office and pushed open the door. The receptionist looked up and smiled.

"Hey, it's me," I asserted. Visiting without being rolled in on a stretcher was foreign.

She grabbed the CD with my records on it and handed it to me, her smirk giving away her mischievous plan.

I noticed a title handwritten in permanent black ink. I had been donned "The Legend"—a moniker earned by my numerous surgeries. One of the nurses had assigned me this appropriate name. I liked it. Who else could compete with my survival record?

My reputation was copious on the advanced cardiac care unit of the hospital also. Frequent stays on six south, the wing reserved for troublesome heart patients, molded me into a regular participant of employee friendships—janitorial staff included.

One visit, after a tough surgery, I was jolted by alarms and heart monitors flashing red. Nurses and aides rushed my room. Pounding faster than a charging bull, my heart rate rose, plunging my blood pressure down to a threatening low.

I gasped for air. The hospital bed was tilted back to prevent shock. My head swooned with dizziness as if I were Dorothy, spinning through the air in *The Wizard of Oz*.

Nurses barked orders at aides and at each other. One, face pale with fear, ran from the room, turning to glance back at me before she disappeared.

After the danger of shock was gone and my heart returned to a normal rate, nurses filed out, picking up debris left in the wake of the battle.

Linda slunk back into my room when everyone had left.

"I am so sorry I ran out," she blurted. "I couldn't take it. I didn't want to lose you, and I was afraid you might die right there." Her face revealed remorse. She bit at her lip nervously. Nurses aren't allowed to leave the room if a patient is in danger of dying.

"I understand," I assured her.

She was deeply concerned and moved. Caring for my heart physically had spilled over into emotionally as well. I felt loved. My heart, to her, was more than muscle and blood vessels.

Fighting to stop my physical heart from breaking, I began to realize the heart is more than a pump—it can be broken emotionally and spiritually.

Can a heart really be broken?

It's considered that a person's heart is the place where the most cherished memories are held. We talk freely about our hearts aching for someone far away, or our hearts going out to others when they are hurting.

How do our hearts go out?

Do we control them with our minds, or are our hearts the central control system? The medical profession considers the heart merely a pump, a mass of muscle, vessels, and networked electrical pathways, pulsing blood through our bodies.

But think about this: Of all the parts in our physical bodies, there is only one heart and we cannot live without it. Many, if not most, of our other body parts and systems can be damaged, destroyed, or shut down and we can still live. Many people are missing multiple physical abilities, yet they live productive and fulfilling lives.

Writers and literary works refer often to the heart, giving it a grand place of distinction. Not simply the physical heart, but the heart as its own entity—its own independent system of emotions, memories, and controls. Here is an example:

Of all the hearts in the world, I've only one to give.
So insecure, a desperate pulse, racing to Your embrace.
That You could want me and seek me, is more than words could ever say.
That You would love me and see in me, a pearl of price thrown away.

A heart like mine, how could it be worthy that You'd find,
A way to redeem this hardened clay, twisted and broken.
O Father God above, the wonder that You love, a heart like mine.

Your holy hands hold me still, shaping my heart anew.
Once vacant shell now reclaimed, offers its praise to You.
The one who searched 'til You found me, a wounded lamb who's gone astray.
You stopped the world to recover me, O Lamb of God, the price You'd pay for ...

I make my promise to do the one thing I can do.
With abandon I can give, every heartbeat to You.[5]

"So insecure, a desperate pulse, racing to your embrace"—those words reach deep into my heart. Painful aching cries out for my physical heart to be healed so I can live comfortably and independently in this world. I want my spiritual heart rejuvenated with strength to make my presence here on earth one of joy and peace, enabling me to rise above the pain.

I feel my heart beating in my chest. It keeps me alive, but somewhere in the deepest part of my soul is another heartbeat that depends on God's redeeming touch. He can get to this spiritual heart only if I let Him.

Wanting to be free of the tangled and painful circumstances I endure is not enough to yield my heart to God. I must determine to give up the fight and let Him intervene for me.

"The LORD will fight for you; you need only to be still" (Ex. 14:14).

I know how hard it is to give it up, to be still. I'm a fighter. Like Jacob, Isaac and Rebekah's son, I walk away with a limp each time I wrestle with God's will.

Jacob was a shepherd in Canaan. His story is recounted in Genesis 25–50. In Genesis 32:25, we read how he wrestled with God all night. He was persistent, even to the point of God touching "the socket of Jacob's hip so that his hip was wrenched."

The story of Jacob in Genesis was a pivotal transformation in Jacob's life and his relationship with God. He realized God's love for him, knowing he should not have lived after seeing God's face. When the wrestling match was done, God changed Jacob's name to Israel, which means "he will rule as God" in Hebrew. This symbolic name also attests of the path to his future generations.

When I wrestle with God, He wins but I grow closer to His plan and purpose for me. He lovingly adds to my spiritual resources so my future will find me with a heart able to withstand the pressures of this world. When I am completely evolved into His care, my life becomes redeemable for any purpose.

"I make my promise to do the one thing I can do. With abandon I can give, every heartbeat to You." With abandon I can give every heartbeat to God, and with faith I can walk securely in His strength. The Old Testament patriarch Abraham was promised much from God, but the trials he endured clouded his days. He chose to remain faithful: "He staggered not at the promise of God through unbelief; but was strong in faith, giving glory to God" (Rom. 4:20 KJV).

Oswald Chambers, in his daily devotional *My Utmost For His Highest,* writes:

> Suppose that you have a deep "well" of hurt and trouble inside your heart, and Jesus comes and says to you, "Let not your heart be troubled ..." (John 14:1). Would your response be to shrug your shoulders and say, "But, Lord, the well is too deep, and even You can't draw up quietness and comfort from it" ... When we get into difficult circumstances, we impoverish His ministry by saying, "Of course, He can't do anything about this." We struggle to reach the bottom of our own well, trying to get water for ourselves. Beware of sitting back, and saying, "It can't be done."[6]

If I can place my life in God's encompassing care, my resolve must include a complete trust in His provision.

One day, a close friend, Nancy Missler, visited with a friend, Melinda, and me. Melinda leaned into the soft couch, tubes protruding from under her neatly pressed blouse. A VAD (ventricular assist device) was attached to her heart through the obtrusive connections woven into her abdomen. The entire contraption resembled a shopping cart filled with exotic electronics. Her controlled heartbeat, audible to ensure everything was working, paced along as we chatted.

Melinda was struggling to live and see her small daughter grow up. Her heart was failing from a genetic disease that had claimed her mom years earlier.

My plight was different—alien forces targeting my heart plagued me.

Both of us sat, carrying on conversation, our hearts tied together by each one's morbid anomaly.

"I wish I could give my heart to either one of you," Nancy shared with tender mercy. "I've lived my life already. I don't need it."

Her offer was genuine. Melinda and I sat silent, restrained from the enormous offer. The heartbeats from her VAD stood alone, accentuating the venerate mood.

Nancy was genuine. She spoke with conviction, willing to sacrifice her own life to give one of us a second chance. Melinda and I witnessed the evidence in her life that she had long ago relinquished control and allowed God to build her up so she could build up those around her.

Her obvious freedom to offer her heart to us was affirmation of her trust in God.

Can Jesus have a broken heart? The concept is penned in an old hymn written in the early 1900s by Thomas Dennis, an assistant pastor in Haslemere, Surrey, England:

> Have you read that He saved the dying thief,
> When hanging on the tree,
> Who looked with pleading eyes and said,
> "Dear Lord, remember me?"
> Have you read that He looked to heaven and said,
> 'Tis finished—'twas for thee?
> Have you ever said, I thank You Lord,
> For giving Thy life for me?
>
> He died of a broken heart for you,
> He died of a broken heart;
> Oh, wondrous love! For you, for me—
> He died of a broken heart.

Genesis 6:6 tells us, "The LORD was sorry that He had made man on the earth, and He was grieved in His heart" (NASB). Dennis's description of Jesus' broken heart echoes the important place our hearts take in our lives, as so often mentioned in the Holy Scriptures.

In her book, *The Heart Speaks*, renowned cardiologist Dr. Mimi Guarneri describes the newly discovered place the heart takes in the body's systems of communication:

> In ancient Greece, Aristotle believed that since the heart was "central, mobile, and hot, and well supplied with structures which served to communicate between it and the rest of the body," it was most suitable to be the seat of the soul.

No matter which view is taken, the heart possesses special attributes that give it supremacy over the brain as the key organ for our survival. It is formed first and stops last. By the sixth week of pregnancy, when the fetus is no bigger than a marble, the cardiac muscle has already formed and begun its initial fluttering movements. Life can continue without the brain, but not once the heart has stopped.

The heart is also exquisitely sensitive to emotions. An angry or fearful thought changes the heart rate variability (HRV) patter—the beat-to-beat variability between each heartbeat—which sets the pace for the brain and respiratory system.

It's long been known that emotions have a physiological impact on our bodies. ... But what if it's not the brain telling the heart what to feel, but the heart informing the rest of the body? What if changing the mind actually involves changing the heart?[7]

With a strong association of the heart's upper role prevalent in the medical community, physicians still haven't realized its potential as God's Word does. Many scriptures refer to the different aspects of the heart. You cannot read about the heart God describes as being the center of our souls without reading about how it also leads and controls our minds, decisions, and lives. It is one of the most talked about subjects in the Bible.

The heart can be instructed:

Do not let kindness and truth leave you; bind them around your neck, write them on the tablet of your heart.

—Prov. 3:3 NASB

The heart can have integrity:

Then God said to him in the dream, "Yes, I know that in the integrity of your heart you have done this, and I also kept you from sinning against Me; therefore I did not let you touch her."

—Gen. 20:6 NASB

The heart can be glad:

Aaron the Levite? I know that he speaks fluently. And moreover, behold, he is coming out to meet you; when he sees you, he will be glad in his heart.

—Ex. 4:14b NASB

The heart can be evil and sinful:

For from within, out of the heart of men, proceed the evil thoughts, fornications, thefts, murders, adulteries, deeds of coveting and wickedness, as well as deceit, sensuality, envy, slander, pride and foolishness. All these evil things proceed from within and defile the man.

—Mark 7:21-23, NASB

The heart contains life:

Watch over your heart with all diligence, for from it flow the springs of life.

—Prov. 4:23 NASB

The heart can be hard:

His heart is as hard as a stone, even as hard as a lower millstone.

—Job 41:24 NASB

The heart can be renewed:

Moreover, I will give you a new heart and put a new spirit within you; and I will remove the heart of stone from your flesh and give you a heart of flesh.

—Ezek. 36:26 NASB

For God, who said, "Light shall shine out of darkness," is the One who has shone in our hearts to give the Light of the knowledge of the glory of God in the face of Christ.

—2 Cor. 4:6 NASB

The scriptures describe the heart as more than simply a physical part of the body. As Dr. Guarneri illustrates, "Forgiveness, optimism, gratitude—these topics would have been dismissed as irrelevant when I was in medical school. Now they are increasingly subjects for serious scientific investigation, as much a part of the heart disease equation as blood cholesterol levels."[8]

During one of my hospital incarcerations, instigated by a near fatal heart attack, a friend came to visit me. She sat on the edge of the bed. Her expression offered concern as she clutched a book in her hands.

"I thought you might like this."

Taking it from her, I read the title: *Waking the Dead* by John Eldredge.

Waking the Dead? What kind of a book is that for someone in the hospital holding on for life?

I accepted it, graciously.

After she left, I placed the book on the window ledge, the ill-boding title glaring up at me with a sneering look.

One especially dreary day, I picked it up and began to read. My expectations dissipated when the words penetrated my dismal mood. Eldredge asserts the glory hidden in all Christians' hearts because of Jesus' redemption and restoration. He propels people to find liberation from this restoring of the heart.

Eldredge, like Dr. Guarneri, speaks of the key role our hearts play physically and spiritually.

> The heart is central. That we would even need to be reminded of this only shows how far we have fallen from the life we were meant to live—or how powerful the spell has been. The subject of the heart is addressed in the Bible more than any other topic—more than works or service, more than belief or obedience, more than money, and even more than worship. Maybe God knows something we've forgotten.

> The Bible sees the heart as the source of all creativity, courage, and conviction. It is the source of our faith, our hope, and, of course, our love. It is the "wellspring of life" within (Prov. 4:23), the very essence of our existence, the center of our being, the fount of our life.

There is no escaping the centrality of the heart. God knows that; it's why He made it the central theme of the Bible, just as He placed the physical heart in the center of the human body. The heart is central; to find our lives, we must make it central again.[9]

Isaiah 27:11 draws a picture of how easily a heart can be broken: "When its twigs are dry, they are broken off and women come and make fires with them. For this is a people without understanding; so their Maker has no compassion on them, and their Creator shows them no favor." The Hebrew word for a bush with fragile, easily broken twigs is *leb shabar*—*leb* representing heart and *shabar* meaning broken.

Two of my favorite verses about God's love to the brokenhearted are found in Psalms and Isaiah:

The LORD is close to the brokenhearted and saves those who are crushed in spirit.

—Ps. 34:18

The Spirit of the Lord God is upon me; because the Lord hath anointed me to preach good tidings unto the meek; he hath sent me to bind up the brokenhearted, to proclaim liberty to the captives, and the opening of the prison to them that are bound.

—Isa. 61:1 KJV

The news is out—doctors are now reporting that the sudden death of someone you love can cause a broken heart. In fact, the condition, "broken heart syndrome," is officially recognized by doctors the world over as reported by cardiologist Ilan Wittstein of the Johns Hopkins University School of Medicine:

Shocking news, such as learning of the unexpected death of a loved one, has been known to cause catastrophic events, such as a heart attack.

Now, researchers at Johns Hopkins have discovered that sudden emotional stress can also result in severe but reversible heart muscle weakness that mimics a classic heart attack. Patients with this condition, called stress cardiomyopathy but known colloquially as "broken heart" syndrome, are often misdiagnosed with a massive heart attack when, indeed, they have suffered from a days-long surge in adrenalin (epinephrine) and other stress hormones that temporarily "stun" the heart.

After observing several cases of "broken heart" syndrome at Hopkins hospitals—most of them in middle-aged or elderly women—we realized that these patients had clinical features quite different from typical cases of heart attack, and that something very different was happening. These cases were, initially, difficult to explain because most of the patients were previously healthy and had few risk factors for heart disease.

While the folklore of "broken heart" syndrome has been around for decades, the prevalence of the condition remains unknown. According to Wittstein, some reports exist, mainly from Japan, and describe similar syndromes, but no biochemical analyses have previously been performed that link the condition to elevated catecholamine levels. The researchers contend that while stress cardiomyopathy is not as common as a typical heart attack, it likely occurs more frequently than doctors realize. They expect its numbers to increase as more physicians learn to recognize the syndrome's unique clinical features. [10]

Understanding the heart physically, emotionally, and spiritually is the beginning of understanding what makes each one of us who we are. Once we find the origin of our own heartaches, we can begin to grasp what we need to overcome the individual trials breaking our hearts.

CHAPTER 2

Chasing the Wind

FIVE MONTHS INTO my waning life with heart disease earned me six heart catheterizations and two additional stents in my arteries. Not knowing when the next blockage may surface forced me to live life cautiously and included new rules and game strategies. Wondering if symptoms were really serious or caused by what I had had for dinner meant making a decision to go to the ER or just to pop a few nitro pills and sleep it off.

It was absurd—baffled by the stream of problems, doctors began scrutinizing my ability to discern real problems from anxiety or stress. My last instructions: "Don't call us unless you have symptoms similar to the first incident in September."

Why do doctors tell heart patients to avoid stress and then add to the rising toll of complications? I was afraid to call—more afraid than having a heart attack. Their doubts instilled a fear of being ridiculed if problems proved to be a false alarm.

But they never did.

OK, I thought, *I'll wait until it gets bad. I won't call them unless I know something is really wrong.*

February 2002, two A.M. Chest pain woke me from a fitful sleep. Piercing pain made its way up into my neck, squeezing me like a boa poised for a kill. I stumbled out of bed. The room's darkness and vague shadows obscured my way. Legs, heavy from lack of circulation, shuffled down the hall to the kitchen.

I reached for the light switch and flicked on the row of track lighting. My eyes squinted from the brightness. There were more than fifteen different prescription bottles on the counter. *Where did I put the nitroglycerin pills?*

I grabbed one by one until I found the nitro, popped off the cap, and quickly placed the chalky pill under my tongue. The initial sting of its explosive properties burned my mouth. I leaned over the counter, waiting for relief.

Once the nitro melted into my bloodstream, a rush of relief cascaded down my chest. The pain lessened. I did this three times but the pain came back like a punching bag returning another blow.

I woke up John and then called the emergency number for my cardiologist's office. When the answering service put me through, an unfamiliar voice asked what was wrong. I trusted he would treat me with respect earned from my extensive list of heart troubles. Instead, his reply panicked my already frazzled nerves.

"You can go to the ER but I don't think it's your heart," he said smugly.

"What do you mean you don't think it's my heart?" I was provoked by his arrogance.

He refused to give me a reason. I dug in my heels and insisted I would not go unless he told me why he didn't think it was my heart. "Why should I go if it isn't my heart?" I retorted. "Why waste everyone's time and money? Besides, I hate going to the ER." We argued back and forth. I pressed him further.

Frustrated, he answered rudely. "I don't want to argue this all night. All right, I'll tell you why I don't think it's your heart. With your history of having symptoms without reason, I think this is psychological. But you can go to the ER anyway."

His reasoning angered me. It was ugly and nasty. I began to cry and handed the phone to John.

A few minutes later, John hung up and took me to the ER. Instead of making the twenty-minute drive to the Heart Institute, I had him take me to our local hospital. *Why not? Nothing is wrong, again.*

At the ER I was poked, prodded, and X-rayed. A dose of morphine and some nitroglycerin were pushed through the IV. Nothing helped.

This time, the ER doctor was a woman with a kind disposition. I liked her. It felt like someone was on my side. Instead of tensing up and bringing on my defensive stature, I relaxed and let her do her job. She made it easy.

All the tests came back normal—but that always seemed to happen. The ER doctor phoned the cardiologist on call and told him she wanted me transported to the Sacred Heart Medical Center ER.

His reply left her nonplussed.

"Oh, just cap off the IV and have her husband drive her. I'm sure she's fine. In fact, send her to admitting instead of the ER. I'll check in on her after she gets to a room."

With protective care like a doting mother, the ER doctor was uneasy about letting me go. By now, I was numb. "Let my husband drive me. I'll be fine."

We drove in silence down the highway to the larger hospital. Hints of morning appeared low in the sky. It was five A.M. by the time we arrived and made our way to the admitting desk. No one was there.

John grabbed a wheelchair and pushed me down the empty hallways, trying to find an admitting clerk. I sat watching the dimly lit pictures on the colorless walls sail by as John desperately searched for anyone who could tell us where to go. Pain throbbed in my chest.

A security guard in his neatly pressed uniform stopped us and asked us where we were going.

"I'm really not sure," John replied, bewildered. "We're supposed to find someone to admit my wife. She's having chest pain."

"Follow me. You'll have to take her to the ER. No one is in admitting until six A.M."

His brisk steps guided us to the ER. A clerk took care of paperwork and John was given a room number to take me up to the sixth floor. Transport personnel were scarce this early and my visits had become frequent and familiar. Like when you marry into a family. After a while, no one caters to you. You're one of the crew. I wondered which nurses were coming in for the day shift.

Once up in the room, check-in procedures began: Medical history? What medicines are you taking? Who is your doctor? Do you have any allergies? What makes the pain worse? Like I really know or care right now, was my sly thought.

Tears welled up in my eyes. I was tired and worn out.

After all the paperwork and blood work were done, I was hooked up to the standard heart monitor that relayed my information remotely to the nurse's station. My heartbeat, EKG, and heart rhythm would be displayed on a TV-like monitor along with those of almost fifty other patients. A nurse sat in front of the pulsating monitors for an entire shift, watching for any abnormalities.

At seven A.M. I sat on the uncomfortable hospital bed feeling as inanimate as the room around me. The doctor on call during the night came into the room and sat next to me. John listened as he spoke in a monotone voice.

"I know you think I don't believe you, but you know, psychological fears can cause you to have symptoms if you are always scared that something could go wrong."

I looked at him and replied defiantly, "When you get a degree in psychology, then I will let you tell me what you think. But I don't believe a cardiologist is required to also major in psychology." After my cutting response, he told me he would be doing a heart catheterization early that afternoon and left. I cried quietly.

Several hours passed before I was prepped and wheeled into the cath lab.

"Please don't put me out completely," I requested of the anesthesiologist. I wanted to know what was happening so I could be the first to sneer when something was found. Sharp poking burned my thigh as medicine was injected to numb my groin area. I shivered from the room's frigid temperature and the anticipation of bad news.

The doctor arrived. Three monitors above my head displayed the inside of my chest. He threaded a catheter through my femoral artery and filled the vessels on top of my heart with dye. I watched anxiously for any indications of a blockage.

Black dye traveled through strands of blood vessels, making their pathway traceable on the screen. But one stopped abruptly, leaving a dead end image where blood could no longer flow. I knew there was a blockage and I knew it was bad. In fact, both my main left artery and a branch coming from it were not filling with dye. I looked at the doctor and his face revealed his regret.

"I guess I should have believed you." He spoke with a heavy sigh and left the room. I never saw him again.

This blockage toppled the stack of repairs and there were no more options except open-heart surgery to bypass my blocked arteries. Tubes delivering medicines that all came together into a main IV site kept me stable but only would suffice until something more could be done.

I felt like I was chasing answers down empty pathways. Repetitive visits, verbally abusive doctors, and failed interventions were tumbling me into an empty abyss. It was like Lewis Carroll's *Alice in Wonderland* when Alice first encounters the White Rabbit:

Down, down, down. Would the fall never come to an end! "I wonder how many miles I've fallen by this time?" she said aloud. "I must be getting somewhere near the centre of the earth."[11]

I always have a problem getting doctors to believe me—always. It's this crying wolf syndrome. Or at least that is what they think. But somthing was always wrong.

Time after time I found myself arguing with staff and attempting to persuade doctors that my symptoms were valid. The stress of proving my cries for help were real out shadowed the fear of a heart attack.

Finally, I asked a Christian psychologist to do an assessment testing of my state of mind so I could prove to the doctors I was not "creating" my symptoms. What a strange request! "Test me to see if I am crazy," I pleaded.

The doctor's building was small and had one counseling room on either side of the foyer. A hard wooden bench sat in the lobby. Its clear varnish, cracked with age, had lost its luster long ago.

Dr. Smith came out of his office and handed me a pamphlet neatly attached to a clipboard. He explained the Minnesota Multiphasic Personality Inventory, or MMPI-2 as it is known, would reveal my way of thinking, outlook on life, and mood, and help determine if I was creating my medical symptoms.

The pamphlet contained 567 true-or-false questions. "There are no right or wrong answers," he instructed. "And don't try to figure it out—you can't."

There was nowhere for me to sit except the lobby with the receptionist facing me. I squirmed on the bench, trying to get comfortable. Every now and then, she would peek up through her reading glasses with a stoic look. I would smile back and continue jotting my answers.

The questions were sometimes absurd and I would giggle as I answered them.

"Do you like to repair door hinges?" How do you answer a question like that? It doesn't even make sense. I tried to figure out how you repair a door hinge but decided I wouldn't like it anyway and answered *false*.

Finishing the last question forty-five minutes later, I placed the pamphlet on the counter. The receptionist took it and informed me a letter would come in the mail in a few weeks. Dr. Smith emerged from his office.

"Done already?" he asked through thick, dark-rimmed glasses. "That was fast."

Fast? Does that mean I answered wrong?

A few weeks later, my letter arrived. I ripped open the envelope. His assessment gave me satisfaction and I beamed with vengeance at his words: "Mrs. Scinto is a high energy, social individual that shows an ability to be assertive when necessary. In my opinion, there is no evidence in my clinical interviews or in the psychological test administered to indicate that she has any psychological etiology for her physical symptoms."

The letter stays folded and securely hidden in my purse. I keep it with me always as a guard against any further heckling from doctors or medical personnel.

One month after my first procedure, symptoms returned. I didn't have my letter to validate my claims. I didn't know I would need a letter.

I phoned the heart doctor's office. After the initial assessment from the secretary, I was passed to a nurse. Her attitude was cold and resistant.

"Your symptoms are normal."

I pressed her, insisting something was wrong.

"Hold on." Classical music droned in my ear.

"Come in tomorrow for another nuclear stress test. Be here by 10:30 A.M. and don't eat anything after midnight tonight."

I obediently followed orders and arrived early the next morning. After everything was finished, the secretary made a follow-up appointment, routinely handed me the reminder card, and walked away.

I walked out of the office—dejected. I felt incomplete. My follow-up appointment wasn't until a month later. I turned around and walked back to the front desk. Three women sat behind the shiny granite counter.

"Excuse me," I asked timidly. "When will I get the results?" All three looked up, their faces perturbed at my question.

"At your follow-up appointment," one answered with a sterile tone.

"But I want to know what they found. I don't feel good. Something is wrong." In anger and frustration, I began to cry. I hated to cry in front of people—especially people who didn't care.

"We have too many patients to deal with. There is no way we can call each one. You will have to wait for your appointment."

My emotions surged, making my skin tingle. I realized she was not going to budge. I left sobbing and wiping my tears like a hurt animal licking its wounds. I was angry. This wasn't about a bad tooth or a broken bone. I almost had died and now something else was wrong.

Those women in the office were so used to the routine, they forgot that new patients are scared, confused, upset, and might need more consideration. I learned the medical community was made up of people, and people will fail.

Many of my appointments would turn into painful disappointments as time after time I was treated with protocol. Even though as a Christian I chose to be patient, enduring, and understanding, I found myself having to fight for proper health care. And, unfortunately, health care in

the United States is on the decline according to a report from University
of Washington Television:

> If the United States spends more on health care than any other nation,
> why isn't our health care system venerated as the best in the world? It
> is questions like these that inspire the work of Dr. Christopher J. L.
> Murray, director of the Institute for Health Metrics and Evaluation
> (IHME) at the University of Washington and professor of global
> health at the UW School of Medicine and School of Public Health
> and Community Medicine.[12]

In Dr. Murray's research of U.S. healthcare, he came to this
conclusion:

> The United States spends the most of any country on health care
> by far, yet we're ranked thirtieth to fortieth in the world in terms of
> quality of public health.

> According to the Centers for Disease Control, there is an average of
> twenty-seven doctors for every ten thousand people in the United
> States. The average in larger cities is much higher, with New York
> averaging thirty-seven doctors per ten thousand people and Washing-
> ton, D.C., averaging as high as seventy-four doctors per ten thousand.
> The dramatic difference of health care in varying geographical areas
> can mean the difference between quality of life for some and life or
> death for others.[13]

Patient satisfaction, as reported in the same article, is no better when
there are higher doctor-to-patient per-capita ratios. Places with more
doctors don't necessarily mean better care.

Why is patient satisfaction so low? Why do more doctors choose
larger cities over rural areas? According to *Public Citizen*:

> Like anyone else, doctors want to live in places where they can earn
> high incomes, enjoy cultural and leisure activities, and send their
> children to good schools. Doctors migrate to states on lists of "Best
> Places to Live": Forty of the top one hundred cities with "strong arts,

cultural programs, and higher education" were in the ten states with the highest per capita number of doctors.[14]

After six years of heart disease, fifty-nine inpatient hospital stays, dozens of doctor appointments and procedures, two open-heart surgeries, a heart transplant, and numerous complications, I can say firsthand that part of the problem lies with a decline in compassion and genuine care. Although doctors are mandated to uphold the Hippocratic Oath, the modern-day interpretation of it has dwindled from its original purpose and an integral part of it has been forgotten: "I will remember that there is art to medicine as well as science, and that warmth, sympathy, and understanding may outweigh the surgeon's knife or the chemist's drug."

God's Word says this about these days on earth: "Because of the increase of wickedness, the love of most will grow cold" (Matt. 24:12).

In Dr. Guarneri's book, the cardiologist comments on the decadent state of patient care and how it affects relationships between doctors and their patients:

Just like the heart, the relationship between a patient and a doctor exists within a cultural context. And in our culture at the present moment, the model is too much technology and not enough time. Therapeutic relationships with empathic family physicians have often been replaced with rushed, impersonal encounters with technicians and machines.

In spite of studies that have long reported that doctors who attend to what their patients tell them have improved clinical outcomes, the constant complaint in patient satisfaction surveys is "My doctor doesn't listen to me!"

Patients aren't alone in finding the quality of medical treatment disturbing. "If I'm not fast, I'm fired," a doctor friend told me.

A heart can't possibly be fathomed simply through catheterization readings or cholesterol levels. The deep stories carved into the hearts of patients can be told only by them.

My patients had changed me. They had shown me the importance of the heart's biography. They had taught me that that coronary disease is physical, spiritual, and emotional.[15]

Dr. Guarneri is paving the way for doctors to combat patient care's regression from being compassionate and intuitive. She also points out the benefits of physicians who look to God for help: "A study published in the journal of *Oncology* found that medical personnel at a cancer center in New York City who described themselves as religious were less subject than other practitioners to emotional exhaustion or 'diminished empathy.'"[16]

Years of dealing with numerous healthcare settings and different physicians and healthcare workers have tempered my patience. Chuck Swindoll, in his Bible Study guide *Hope in Hurtful Times, A Study of 1 Peter*, wants our focus not to be on the unfair treatment but on what God would have us do when we are treated wrongly:

> And the natural tendency of the human heart is to fight back against unfair and unreasonable treatment. But Peter's point is that seeking revenge for unjust suffering is a sign of self-appointed lordship over one's affairs.[17]

Swindoll's advice?

> If you're enduring suffering right now, especially unjust suffering, it can be a dizzying experience. To keep your balance in those times, when things are swirling around you, it's important to find a fixed point and focus on it.[18]

Many painful experiences I continuously endured through all the medical issues and procedures bring me back to the verses I listed in the beginning of this book, the anchors that keep me from drowning in self-pity and anger:

> Beware of turning to evil, which you seem to prefer to affliction.
> —Job 36:21

Do not grieve, for the joy of the LORD is your strength.

—Neh. 8:10

Deal courageously, and the LORD shall be with the good.

—2 Chron. 19:11b KJV

God wants me to be courageous. He does not want me to grieve, and He does not want me to choose evil over affliction. Many of us going through difficult times right now need to have a heavenly perspective. In James 4:13-14, the Lord shows us how our lives are not something we can hold onto: "Now listen, you who say, 'Today or tomorrow we will go to this or that city, spend a year there, carry on business and make money.' Why, you do not even know what will happen tomorrow. What is your life? You are a mist that appears for a little while and then vanishes."

The King James Version calls our lives a "vapor" which Webster's defines as "something unsubstantial or transitory."[19]

If our lives are a mist or vapor, we cannot hold on to them, we cannot mold our future, and we cannot control when our lives begin or end. These three concepts—do not turn to evil, be joyful, and be courageous—have sustained me through the many letdowns in the past years, and those that continue to this day. I sought help from doctors in my home state of Washington, and in San Diego, Phoenix, New York, Pennsylvania, and as far away as Canada and Italy.

When my blockages first began, stents—small coiled, metal supports to hold open coronary arteries—were the best choice over open-heart surgery. Often, however, these stents would block up due to scar tissue from the grueling procedure of clearing out the original blockages. On the horizon were "medicated" stents that were coated with a medicine to prevent "restenosis" or recurrence of blockages after corrective surgery on a coronary artery. The U.S. Food & Drug Administration approved these drug-coated stents in 2003, but there were many times before they were approved that I was in desperate need of their technology.

In Washington State, January is frigid and the cold snow falls without mercy. Even if the weather had not been designated officially as a blizzard, we were having one the day I got admitted again for chest pain.

I settled into my room and was unpacking my bag. I kept one ready at home like a pregnant woman. "It's time, honey," I would chide when I knew I would be admitted.

My cell phone sat silently on the dresser. It was dinnertime and no one knew I had been admitted. That would come later. Informing everyone of another hospital visit was monumental. Explaining why was just as tiring.

After getting a large, poorly designed hospital gown draped over my shoulders, I reached for the cloth ties. They were hard to find and to figure out which one matched. My arms were twisted around my back, trying to make a knot, when the cell phone rang. I let go of the flimsy strings and reached for the phone.

"Cindy Scinto?" the abrupt, New York-sounding voice asked.

"Yes."

"This is Dr. Tierstein. I heard about your case and am willing to place a medicated stent in your coronary artery if you are having another blockage. The only setback is there are many protocol requirements, so you will have to be here at the hospital by ten A.M. tomorrow to be eligible for the medicated stent."

Dr. Tierstein, based out of Scripps clinic in San Diego, was part of a three-man, doctor/friend team originating in New York City. All were audacious New Yorkers—feisty, arrogant, and brilliant. I already had encountered one of his cohorts in New York when Dr. Jeffrey Moses had worked on me.

Dr. Moses was heading up trials with drug-coated stents for Johnson & Johnson. He had had offered to help me back in August 2002 and performed a procedure that later saved my life (you will read more about this in chapter 3).

Dr. Tierstein's offer sent me into a whirlwind of determination.

"I will be there," I promised.

The admitting nurse came in and watched me dance around, her face reflecting confusion and concern.

With rapid-fire phrases, I explained the proposition and told her I wanted to be discharged immediately.

"But I just got you in the system," she said. "If you sign yourself out, you not only take the chance of having a heart attack, you will be considered AMA by your insurance."

"What is AMA?" I asked her.

"'Against Medical Advice,' and the insurance company can choose to deny payment for your time here."

"Show me where to sign," I insisted. "I have to go."

She turned reluctantly to grab the paperwork from the nurses' station.

I got hold of the twisted hospital gown, now jumbled into a mass around my shoulders, and threw it down on the bed. By time the nurse returned, I was dressed and ready.

When John and I left the hospital it was six P.M. There were no more flights to San Diego leaving from Spokane. But there was a flight from Portland to San Diego the next morning at five A.M. He booked two tickets—our son, Jonathan, would stay with a friend. We would have to leave that night and drive through the storm to get to Portland in time.

Snow blew sideways and pelted our faces as we loaded the van. The wind was bitter cold and the street slippery under our feet. We drove to our friend's house and pulled up the snow-covered driveway.

"Here, Angie, put this somewhere safe." I handed her a thick envelope with "Our Wills" scrolled across the front.

"In case something happens to John and me, all the instructions are in here along with our wills." She looked into my eyes but I turned to hug Jonathan.

Will I be back to see him?

We drove away in the heavy snow.

The freeway was packed down and covered with ice. Our headlights reflected off the thick snow, blanketing the windshield like a loosely crocheted afghan. John drove into the storm, keeping our van steady. He watched forward, staring ahead.

Occasionally, we could see the outline of a vehicle that had slid off the road and quickly had been taken over by mounds of fresh snow. A UPS truck sat in the middle divider, leaning dangerously to one side.

I watched out the frozen window, wanting to help. It was because of me we were in this crazy storm driving to Portland in the middle of the night—to hopefully catch a flight to San Diego and maybe get a chance at a medicated stent that might help me.

I gasped as John veered back into our lane after the van almost careened off the road.

"Please go lie down in the back before you really do have a heart attack!" he insisted.

I climbed to the back seat and tried to lie down but apprehension snapped me up. I returned to the front and promised I would calm down.

Two hours into the trip, the foreboding snow changed to a dense fog enclosing us in a dark, gray cocoon. The only thing visible was the van's silver hood reflecting back the glow from our headlights.

I remembered when I was ten years old and my parents drove me to a camp for diabetics. It was a summer night, but we were stuck in the thick, wet fog of New England. My dad drove through, following a tractor-trailer's taillights in front of us. My mom sat in the front passenger seat, fingering the baby-blue-colored beads she carried in her purse as she prayed the rosary.

While she prayed, I held on to the seat cushion, my fingers clutching the vinyl-piped edge. I was worried we would have an accident. It was my fault I was a diabetic. It was my fault they had to take me to a special camp.

And now it was my fault we were on this trip. Not wanting to distract John, I kept my thoughts to myself.

After another two hours, we were driving along the Columbia River on the border of Oregon. A hint of sunrise peered through the clouds and the fog dissipated into a new morning. It was 3:30 A.M. We had to be at the airport by four A.M. to check in.

I watched each sign on the highway, comparing it to my map.

"Looks like three more miles," I assured John, folding the half-torn map into a small rectangle.

Signs appeared for the Portland airport. The green reflective backboard and shiny white lettering, framed against gray skies, caught my eye.

John got off the exit and we pulled into the parking lot. He took both our bags and we headed for the shuttle stop. I was flushed and hot from the anxiety and fear that we would miss the plane. The damp Oregon air cooled my face.

We reached the gate before the last passenger boarded. Once on the plane and in our seats, I leaned my head back, closed my eyes, and took a deep breath. *Oh, Lord, let me survive this flight without a heart attack.*

We both drifted off to sleep.

Two and a half hours later, the plane landed in San Diego. The mad rush started again as we scanned the luggage carousel for our bags. John made a break through the dense groups of people huddled around the edge of the moving conveyer. He spotted ours together on the shiny metal belt. Once he had the bags in his hands, we hurried to the rental car desk.

Our friend Keith met us there. We would follow his car to the hospital to save time looking for it ourselves. It was nine A.M. and we had to be there by ten A.M.

We got on the freeway and followed his SUV in the California traffic. I sat in the back seat so I could rearrange my luggage to pack an overnight bag for the hospital. There was no time to think about the nagging pain pushing on my chest.

Furiously, I transferred items from one bag to another with one hand and used my other hand to dial my cell phone. I tucked it under my chin when it started to ring.

"Angie? Hi! It's me, Cindy. We made it here safely. How is Jonathan?"

"He's fine. Are you on the way to the hospital?"

Before I could answer, John steered the car sharply off the freeway and stopped on the shoulder.

"Get out!" he yelled frantically at me.

"What are you doing?" I asked him.

"The car caught fire! Get out!"

"Angie, the car is on fire. I have to go. Don't worry." I hung up abruptly.

We grabbed our bags and jumped out of the car. Thick, black smoke rose from the undercarriage. I watched cars on the freeway whiz by unaffected as our rental fumed. The caustic smell burned our noses.

Keith pulled over and ran toward us.

"What happened? I looked back and you were gone. Then I saw you pulled over and the smoke from the car—"

"No time to figure it out," John said. He called the rental agency.

"Our rental caught fire. It's on the freeway between exits 20 and 21. I have to get my wife to the hospital. The keys are in the ignition." He hung up.

We got into Keith's SUV. I looked back to see the smoky scene and thought how ludicrous it was for John to call the rental agency and succinctly report a burning vehicle we abandoned. He was calm and focused.

Thank God.

I had enough time to call Angie and tell her we were OK before we arrived at the hospital. "Don't tell Jonathan what happened. I don't want him to worry more."

The lush hospital entrance was lined with palm trees and brightly colored, exotic plants. The ocean was less than two blocks away. I loved the beach. Sounds of waves thundering to the shore caught my ear. The smell of saltwater tickled my nose. I glanced past the road and saw blue-gray water dotted with white caps. *Oh, how cruel to be so close to the warm beach and entering a cold harsh hospital instead.*

I checked in at the front desk and was taken to a prep room. The process began like always but this time I was excited about a medicated stent being used. Especially after how hard it had been to get there.

When I woke up an hour after the heart cath was done, I was back in a room to recuperate. John and Keith came in, looking at me with prosaic expressions.

"You didn't get a medicated stent," John explained. "The doctor said there was no blockage to repair. You were having coronary spasms that can feel like a blocked artery but everything was OK."

Medication was doled out to calm my heart and relieve the spasms, and I was sent home that afternoon. We stayed two days before traveling home to Spokane.

I moped around afterward, dragging myself through each day. *No blockage? Making a mad rush to get to San Diego for nothing?*

I was disappointed and frustrated, not that I didn't have a blockage but that I couldn't understand why this was happening. I was chasing cures, looking for an end to the madness.

I felt like the woman who touched Jesus' garment:

A large crowd followed and pressed around him. And a woman was there who had been subject to bleeding for twelve years. She had suffered a great deal under the care of many doctors and had spent all she had, yet instead of getting better she grew worse. When she heard about Jesus, she came up behind him in the crowd and touched his cloak, because she thought, "If I just touch his clothes, I will be healed." Immediately her bleeding stopped and she felt in her body that she was freed from her suffering.

At once Jesus realized that power had gone out from him. He turned around in the crowd and asked, "Who touched my clothes?"

"You see the people crowding against you," his disciples answered, "and yet you can ask, 'Who touched me?'"

But Jesus kept looking around to see who had done it. Then the woman, knowing what had happened to her, came and fell at his feet and, trembling with fear, told him the whole truth. He said to her, "Daughter, your faith has healed you. Go in peace and be freed from your suffering."

—Mark 5:25-34

What I was doing wrong?

My attempts to go to Canada to get a medicated stent ended after I found out their government-funded healthcare would not accept my insurance. I even contacted a cousin in Italy to find out if the University of Pisa Medical School would accept me as a patient. But unfavorable relations with the pharmacological companies in the U.S. had created a bad relationship with Americans. They would not see me.

I chased after the doctor in San Diego and his cohort in New York and saw the third member of this alliance in Seattle at the University Hospital. None of them had any answers for me.

Like the woman who touched Jesus' garment, I longed for a way to tap into God's healing power. She had an incurable condition and desperately wanted Jesus to heal her.

Sometimes we feel our problems will keep us from God—we undermine His deity when we doubt His ability to heal us. It is more about when and how He will heal. I may not have seen an answer to my desire to be healed at that time, but later on I would realize His plan was not set to my agenda.

During one of my frequent hospitalizations, I was in the shower getting ready to have yet another nuclear stress test. Exhausted by the constant testing and procedures, I prayed, "Lord, please, either heal me and take away the pain or show the doctors what needs to be done so I can get over this and get on with life."

Immediately, but gently, the Lord replied, "I cannot heal you until you are ready to accept how I choose to heal you. And I am not finished yet."

"But I have prayed that I will accept whatever you choose," I said with surety. I pondered my reaction the next week, wondering if I had given my will to God.

Shortly after this word from God, I was faced with His promise.

It was four A.M., and a tall, dark, bellowing technician came into my room to do an EKG. I always marvel at the timing in a hospital. Right when you sink off into a much-needed reprieve of sleep, someone has to take blood, check your temperature, or do something else nonessential.

As he did the EKG, we talked about open-heart surgery. He had survived the same surgery a few years prior and touted how much better he was. "It was the best thing I ever did," he said. "I feel great now."

After he left, I lay there in the solemn shadows and, finally, it made sense. I knew at that moment that God wanted all of me. He is a jealous God and nothing can come between Him and me. Nothing.

"OK, Lord. If you want me to accept however You choose to heal me, I will. I will go into this angioplasty singing!" I was scheduled that day to have one to determine if I needed bypass surgery.

I called John as soon as it was morning and told him not to worry—I was joyful and happy. Surgery would go fine. Everything was great. I sensed he wasn't as convinced. He was worn out.

That morning I was wheeled into the catheterization lab for the angioplasty. I was beaming. The nurses all knew me and had upbeat music playing—fifties music. There was an air of jocularity as the doctor arrived.

He obviously wasn't as happy as I felt.

I was having chest pain even though I was being pumped with massive doses of medications. It got quiet as he entered my heart with the catheter. The monitor pulsated with the beating of my heart. This time he searched much longer than before. When he was done, he turned the monitor toward me. There was no blockage to be found. All clear! I was elated.

"God healed my arteries!" I told everyone.

John was happy—everyone was happy. I felt great!

Later that day, the doctor came into my room and suggested antidepressants for my anxiety.

"But I'm not anxious," I appealed to him.

"I've been doing this for thirteen years," he informed me. "People say they are not anxious but they really are and don't know it. At least the antidepressants will help you sleep."

"But I sleep fine," I continued to protest. "Will antidepressants help my heart?"

"No," he answered.

"Then I refuse them. I don't need them."

I was humiliated. He obviously thought my problems were in my head. Did everyone else think this was psychological? My inferiority complex dampened the happiness.

Part of accepting how God healed me was again suffering the embarrassment of a doctor accusing me of creating my symptoms. I hated the feeling of being treated like an unstable basket case.

I confronted the doctor about the tests that showed a blockage before the heart cath. He made excuses about the way the results were read and interpreted.

I swallowed my pride and faced the belittlement.

God did heal me, as He would on many occasions.

When we pray, we need to ask what we need without an agenda. God will answer our petitions in His perfect way. His ways are not ours.

But even after this miraculous healing, blockages continued to form and more stents and procedures were performed. Open-heart surgery became inevitable.

It was February 2002, and I was in the hospital again.

"I'm going down to the cafeteria to get some coffee." John shuffled out of the room.

A few minutes later, the door opened and a well-dressed, debonair man walked in.

"I'm Dr. Icenogle, the heart surgeon." He sat in a chair, paging through my chart.

I sat on the bed, wishing John would get back to hear what he had to say.

"Your main artery is about to collapse. If it goes down—you go with it unless you let me do a double bypass on your heart."

This was the first time I experienced his blatant way of delivering awful news. A silent pause stilled the room. I knew he was serious and surgery was unavoidable.

"I'm a Christian and I pray about each operation I perform. Usually I get a sense of how it's going to turn out. I can't seem to tell with you." He scribbled notes on the progress sheet in my chart.

His mannerism was so flat I normally would have found it disconcerting but there was a confidence about him. I knew he was serious and capable.

"You talk to your husband about it, but don't wait too long."

He was only gone a minute when John got back. I told him about the option of surgery and what Dr. Icenogle had said.

John agreed it had to be done.

The surgery was scheduled for Monday.

John stared helplessly from a pale-blue cushioned chair as nurses in brightly colored uniforms traveled around my room. Each had a mission. One pushed syringes of medicines through the intrusive needle in my arm while another hung clear plastic bags of prescribed liquids to be routed through a multitude of tubing.

Anxious thoughts pelted my mind as I was prepped for a double-bypass.

Lonny, a tall, slender RN, barked orders at aides to hurry. "The surgeons are already in the OR. Let's move it, people." She was my favorite nurse. Tough and commanding with her staff, she switched gears once she entered my room.

"How's the chest pain?" she gently asked.

"It's getting worse."

John watched as Lonny grabbed a syringe and shot medicine into my IV. A few seconds later, John's profile faded to shadowy darkness as my body relaxed into the sedative. *Oh, Lord, please help me.* Thoughts of chest pain were replaced by worry and fear. *Will I be strong enough to survive this surgery?*

After orderlies wheeled me down to the pre-op room, John leaned over and tenderly kissed my forehead. He whispered a prayer into my ear. With teary eyes I assured him it would be OK.

The long, dim hallway swallowed his silhouette as John made his way to the family waiting room. He rounded the corner and was gone. I pictured the well-known scene in my mind. Anemic colored walls illuminated by fluorescent lights held clues of former residents: a red crayon mark from a child's play, coffee stains running down behind worn end tables, and faded paint told of the long history of visitors.

I pictured John slumped against the familiar wall, staring blankly at the worn pages of an outdated magazine.

Back in the OR, attendants dressed in green scrubs hurried to make way for the surgeon who would weave borrowed vessels—one from my leg and one from my chest area—attaching them to blocked arteries around my heart. The room was icy cold. A flat, steel operating table pressed against the thin sheets under me, sending shivers through my body.

The anesthesiologist looked down through a blue surgical mask and explained about medicine to make me sleep, but before his sentence was finished, my eyes closed against the powerful force of the anesthesia.

Three hours later, Dr. Icenogle entered the waiting room, his drab green OR attire stained with sweat.

"It was a difficult surgery," he explained to John. "But she's in recovery and her vital signs are stable. She will sleep for a few hours and then you can go in and see her."

John's face was stoic, but his shoulders slumped with relief at the good news. Friends who gathered to support him hugged and cried, each one feeling the battle for my life had been won.

Later, John was alone by my side in the recovery room. He leaned against the wall to grab some rest. With a jump, he awoke to blaring alarms. My vital signs had dropped to dangerous levels, triggering the monitors to scream with erratic beeping and blinking red lights. Nurses charged in and the quiet room ignited with an outbreak of commotion.

John was escorted out with instructions to again confine himself to the family waiting room. He stood at the entrance and watched personnel running down the hall to the post-op area. His body trembled with fear.

Shortly after, Dr. Icenogle entered the waiting room, his chalky white face wrinkled with concern.

"There's massive internal bleeding somewhere. I have to go in and find it. She's in critical condition and with all the blood loss, I have to tell you—I'm not sure I can save her."

John stared at Dr. Icenogle, eyes fixed on his expression, hoping to see some assurance.

"You can walk with us as we take her back to the OR." Dr. Icenogle put his hand on John's shoulder.

Two attendants rolled the stretcher back into the pre-op area. John followed until he was at the OR doors and could go no farther.

"I'll do my best," Dr. Icenogle promised.

The surgery was successful and I was admitted to the ICU. While I was in a coma, nurses and doctors took turns adjusting equipment and measuring heart function. John was at my bedside. His head lay on his folded arms. He held my hand and hoped my fingers would tighten around his. Instead, my limp, lifeless body was still except for my chest rhythmically rising up and down with a respirator's help.

John lifted his head and leaned closer to my face. He listened to the swoosh of air being forced through the respirator's tubing. He held back a sob and whispered into my ear, "I love you."

Later that night, when I came to, my eyes opened to see John looking down at me. He never left the room. He wanted to be there when I awoke. His calm expression was reassuring and although I had no idea what had happened, I knew I would be OK.

The next day, salty tears ran down my cheeks as I looked into John's weary face.

"I heard you say 'I love you,' and those words gave me the determination to fight."

"Did you hear the nurses and Dr. Icenogle talking to you?" he asked. "They tried to get you to wake up and breathe on your own."

"No, I heard you—no one else."

While I was in the intensive care unit, John read to me from the Bible. My son Jonathan had sent a message for him to read Psalm 86.

"It will help you, Mom," he said. "It's about God fighting for you."

Surgeries and procedures were done to keep me alive and hopefully give me what is often coldly termed as "quality of life," but my health continued to degrade. At one point, my medical insurance company assigned me a case manager named Carole.

My first impression at the idea was annoyance. "Oh no, they don't! I don't want anyone to report to or explain my problems to." The last thing I wanted was someone else meddling with my appointments and needs.

Clouded by exhaustion and skepticism, I thwarted my insurance company's efforts and would not answer Carole's phone calls. But her persistence irked me, so I finally decided to answer her next call and make it clear that I did not need or want her help.

If I had had any foresight about how my case manager would play into what happened next, I never would have been so defensive about her contacting me. The instinct to avoid any more aspects of the process I was fumbling through, along with the urge to minimize more requirements, caused me to be mistrustful.

Late one afternoon, the phone rang. Its sound was like a dagger through my head. Noises annoyed me and noises that required my attention were especially hated.

I looked at the caller ID. It was Carole.

Although hesitant, I picked up the phone and we began to talk. She was surprisingly pleasant and I didn't feel threatened. Shortly into the conversation, she convinced me to become part of the insurance company's patient-care assistance program.

A few days later, I received the paperwork and woefully filled out the forms. "They want to make sure I don't cost them extra money," I mumbled as I placed the envelope in the mailbox.

Carole and I talked once a week. Sometimes she helped me with insurance claims, appointments, or medical concerns. My cynical conspiracy theory settled down a bit, and I began to trust her.

One week, a phone call from Carole made a life-saving difference for me—something I would not expect from a case manager.

"Cindy, this is Carole." The excitement in her voice was like someone calling to let me know I had won a million dollars.

"I found a clinical trial on the Web. It looks like you fit the requirements."

The protocol was for an experimental drug used to grow new arteries in heart patients with no options left. At that time, I was one of the no-option patients. Open-heart surgery would no longer help get much needed blood to my worn-out heart. My main artery was completely lined with metal stents that had been dubbed by my cardiologist as "full metal jacket." And when asked about how many times he had cleared out blockages, his reply was, "We have gone where no man has gone before."

Medications to keep my heart from overworking kept me in a vegetative state—a short walk from my bedroom to the kitchen was monumental.

The trial Carole found was for CardioVascular BioTherapeutic's (a pharmaceutical company in Las Vegas) Cardio Vascu-Grow, known as FGF-1, a growth hormone that produces new blood vessel growth around the heart. Dr. Thomas Stegmann engineered this new technology in Germany and it was already changing the lives of many people in his country. I immediately got online and read the trial's requirements. Scrolling down the computer screen, I speed-read to make sure I wasn't going to be disappointed—again.

That week, I went in to see my cardiologist. I showed him the requirements.

"This is amazing," he said as he read through the printout. "It would be great if you could make the trial."

We began the long, arduous application process.

Clinical medical trials require enormous piles of paperwork and testing. We worked on it for weeks—records to be sent, lab work, eye exams, echocardiograms, X-rays—until I thought the stress of waiting to find out if I would be accepted could kill me before they saved me.

One month after the process began, I received a phone call that I had been accepted. I wanted to jump up and down! Sedatives kept me dispassionate on the outside but inside I was bursting with hope. *Maybe now I can get my life back.*

The surgery and treatment were scheduled for December at Penn State Milton S. Hershey Medical Center in Hershey, Pennsylvania. The local newspaper in Spokane ran a story titled "She needs a Christmas miracle":

> A day without heart problems is almost unthinkable for the forty-three-year-old Spokane Valley woman. She spends much of her day sedated on a couch because the excitement of everyday life is too much. Her kitchen counter resembles a small pharmacy.
>
> But Scinto is not taking her cardiac problems lying down. Two months ago when doctors told her they had tried everything, the mother from Greenacres got on the Internet and enrolled in an experimental cloned gene program in Hershey, Pennsylvania.
>
> Scinto said the procedure is her Christmas miracle. Her Spokane cardiologist, Donald Canaday, considers the experimental procedure a final alternative.
>
> "The reason we got her into gene therapy is because it is the only thing that hasn't been done," Canaday said.
>
> "We are just so grateful for this holiday miracle," Scinto said. "Even though we will spend Christmas and New Years alone in Pennsylvania, we are just happy that I may get some strength and health back."[20]

The air travel to Hershey was dangerous. There is nowhere to go if you have a heart attack at 30,000 feet! I medicated myself with tranquilizers so I would stay calm and sleepy. The flights were on time and we arrived to a snowy welcome.

December is a great time of year to visit Hershey if you are able to go out and enjoy the chocolatey town. Every afternoon, after three P.M., the wind would change direction and no matter where you were, you could smell freshly milled chocolate. But I was there for a miracle, not a chocolate bar.

After a week of additional testing and prep, the surgery was done and the FGF-1 was injected into my blocked main artery. I felt like a queen with troves of workers gathered around tending to all my needs. Doctors and surgeons watched me intently, waiting for a sign the experimental agent was working.

It did work—faster than anyone expected. I went from a wheelchair-bound invalid to being energetic and walking a brisk mile five days after surgery. John, Jonathan, and I remained in Hershey five more weeks to be sure I was healed up and to watch my progress.

News reached the papers two months later that there had been a 100 percent turnaround. One headline screamed: "She's Too Well!"

"This looks beautiful," Boehmer said about the images from Scinto's last heart X-ray. Iodine—the dark liquid that illuminates blood flow on an X-ray—shot freely through her artery and venal bypass. He grinned.

"Aw, man … can't beat that," Boehmer said.

The X-rays showed a vessel had sprouted and formed a loop around a blockage in her artery, sparing Scinto from a heart attack. Another vessel appears to have restored blood flow to a bypass that had become blocked. Her stress test was normal. "This is the point in clinical care when we usually claim victory," Boehmer said from the office at Penn State Milton S. Hershey Medical Center.

Scinto had improved so much by that June 7 visit that she would no longer be eligible for her experimental treatment, which is being reviewed by the U.S. Food and Drug Administration. In December, doctors at Hershey injected a synthetic protein into her heart.

"Right now, she's too well," Boehmer said.[21]

Within five days, this miraculous growth hormone grew new coronary vessels around my failing heart. There were no side effects, no health issues—just a chance to live again.

Dr. Stegmann, professor of surgery and a world-renowned cardiovascular surgeon, began researching the potential of angiogenesis in Germany in the early nineties. His work led to the first clinical trials of the FGF-1 growth hormone in the United States, the one of which I was a part in 2003. Dr. Stegmann expressed his own experience after hearing of my story:

Under normal circumstances, a physician always sees his patient after surgery. He or she takes time to discuss how the surgery went with the patient's family and loved ones. This practice was implemented so long ago that it is hard to say when it came to pass. What is strange for me is that a patient I did not even know went through my U.S. clinical trial, using a procedure I pioneered.

I had no idea how great her suffering really was. When I started my own clinical trials in Germany, I knew the patients—most of them were well over fifty years old and after the procedure, I was able to talk with all of them. They all were diagnosed with Acute Coronary Heart Disease and had reached the point of "No Option" or "Zero Option," meaning additional coronary artery stents or bypass surgery would not help get blood and oxygen back into their hearts. Most of them truly had about two years left to live.

I knew our protein therapy worked and was not surprised to hear of its success, but listening to the story of such a young woman, only in her forties and just starting her life, and learning that my discovery kept her alive, somehow at that particular moment struck me as one of the most profound moments in my own life. Right there and then it clearly awakened within my mind the reality of my purpose. Here I was, sitting and quietly observing this woman when just like opening your eyes to a new day, I understood that everything I have been fighting for, all with the hopes of finding a way to stop the unnecessary suffering, finally was happening. This therapy worked and did actually take the pain and suffering away from those in misery due to heart disease, and although it was not a cure, it can help those in need.

To actually meet this woman who has gone through so much, as she stood in front of me with her one desire, to shake my hand, the hand of the man she claims saved her life, was overwhelming and heartfelt to me. Even after all the years of being a heart surgeon, knowing that I finally found the way to help stop the pain, allowing people like

Cindy to get back to her life and try to have some normalcy that so many of us take for granted, made it one of the most wonderful days of my life.[22]

As I recount this experimental procedure and how it came to pass, I think of my hesitancy when I first got news of a case manager becoming part of my life. How tragic the thought that if I had not had the experimental surgery—being the third person in the United States to have it done—I probably would not have lived long enough to receive a heart transplant in July 2005.

Although the procedure did not allow me a complete recovery, it was part of two miracles in my journey.

Three months after the experimental injection of FGF-1, another massive blockage was found in my main coronary artery that would have caused a fatal heart attack if the new vessels had not been there. And, of course, the new vessels brought much needed blood flow to my heart, allowing me to live long enough to wait for a donor heart to be available.

After each procedure or surgery, I often would chase the dream that I was going to recover completely.

Alone one day, I cried and pleaded with God, "Please heal me so I can serve You once again."

For years before my illness I had been part of many events at church. I scurried from one area to the next, from changing diapers in the nursery to playing flute on the worship team. I wanted it all back.

God's reply was precise: "You *are* serving Me."

I had to rediscover where it was that God wanted me to be and how He wanted me to serve Him. Chasing a healing, and pushing for answers to prayers I demanded instead of presented to God, only would rob me of His will for my life.

Joni Eareckson Tada, in her book *Joni*, prayed a similar prayer:

Lord, I know now that You have something planned for my life. But I need help understanding Your will. I need help in knowing Your Word. Please, God, do something in my life to help me serve You and know Your Word.[23]

Joni's prayer was answered. Although she too chased avenues to regain the ability to walk and desired for God to heal her, she found much more to her life through what He provided in place of the losses she had suffered.

In Jeremiah 36 we read about the evil King Jehoiakim and how he burned the scrolls containing the words from God that Jeremiah and his scribe Baruch so painstakingly had written over twenty years.

But the word of the Lord came to Jeremiah and starting in verse 28 we read:

> Take another scroll and write on it all the words that were on the first scroll, which Jehoiakim king of Judah burned up.

Jeremiah did this and more:

> So Jeremiah took another scroll and gave it to the scribe Baruch son of Neriah, and as Jeremiah dictated, Baruch wrote on it all the words of the scroll that Jehoiakim king of Judah had burned in the fire. And many similar words were added to them (Jer. 36:32).

Jill Briscoe, in her book *Faith Enough to Finish*, poses this poignant question about Jeremiah and Baruch:

> Would they have faith enough to finish? How would they respond to the voice of God? How would you have responded? Would you start all over again, or would you quit? ... Jeremiah handed Baruch another scroll and began all over again. They did it again. Yes, they did it again! Now that's faithfulness![24]

Fire and an evil king erased years of work, yet Jeremiah and Baruch were willing to start over and go further.

Chasing the wind can be futile or it can lead us to press on. Make God the wind you press into, and He will hold you up to continue your life as He planned it for you. There is much more ahead.

CHAPTER 3

Isn't It Amazing?

Isn't it amazing what a prayer can do,
When it all seems hopeless it'll pull you through.
Isn't it amazing how a broken heart grows strong,
When every now and then that
Someone special comes along.[25]

AGAIN, I WAS rolled into the heart catheterization lab's operating room, where a technician was waiting to hook me up to equipment and medications. Big, bad Dave came to the holding area to get me.

"When I saw 'Cindy Scinto' on the schedule, I had to come get you myself," he commanded. "Why are you here?"

His expression was serious—not gruff and comical like it normally was. This was heart catheterization number thirty-four and Dave had been the attending nurse for most of them. He was known not to smile, but I was one patient who normally could coax him into a mischievous grin.

"Is Carol here?" I asked. "Don't take it personally," I assured one of the nurses, "I just love Carol."

"Carol's here," answered Dave. "In fact, she changed her shift so she could be here for you."

Carol was another nurse who had attended most of my heart procedures. Her wispy blonde hair, bright eyes, and broad smile always comforted me amid the operating room busyness before I was put to sleep. Her calming hand stroked my forehead as I was lulled off by the anesthesia. It was her concern and comforting presence that I saw last, and it stayed with me when I woke up.

Once a year, in July, I have to go through testing and a heart catheterization to be sure my donor heart is doing OK. But here I was in May, having a procedure to see if I really had a blockage in one of the vessels on my heart's left side.

For a few weeks I had been having chest pain and fatigue. A nuclear stress test a few days prior had shown decreased blood flow on the left side. For a transplant of barely three years, that is bad news. If the vessels around my heart already were starting to block up, it could mean whatever was originally wrong with me had started to attack this new heart.

I had e-mailed friends and family the night before and asked everyone to pray for a miracle. I asked them to pray it was a fluke and there really was no blockage. With the symptoms I was having and a positive nuclear stress test, the odds of not having a blockage were slim and, short of a miracle, I would be facing some discouraging news.

I also called Charlotte, my heart donor's mom, the night before: "Charlotte, I have to have a heart catheterization. It looks like I may have a blockage in one of the vessels. But don't worry, I am going to tell the doctor to make sure he takes care of Danielle's heart. I won't let anything happen to 'our' heart."

Charlotte assured me she would be praying. We were in this together. She lost her daughter to a tragic accident—but I gained a new chance at life through her daughter's act of kindness as an organ donor. (Read about my heart donor and her family in chapter 7.)

The last words I spoke before my eyes shut were to my cardiologist performing the procedure: "Dr. Canaday, you'd better take care of this heart! It's been through enough. Let's make Danielle proud!"

I awoke from the anesthesia back in my room to good news. No blockage! Although the heart had an area of stiffness and elevated pressure, there was *no blockage*.

The stiffness is common for a heart that has been damaged, repaired, placed on ice, and then transplanted into another person. Medication was prescribed and more time in my garden suggested. I knew God had healed me. I knew God had heard the prayers of many and healed the blockage.

Some of the hospital personnel explained it away as an inaccurate test result, but I wouldn't let anyone steal the miracle God had performed! In fact, one of my doctors and my heart transplant nurse/coordinator attributed the results to a healing from God. Healing is a controversial subject for many, and for some it's an outright impossibility. But I knew God had healed my heart.

Many people have heard about *healing*. The subject either can spur someone on to seek God's will or it can become a catalyst for heated arguments. Often, people are made to feel inadequate if the healing they pray for does not come. Some consider it an issue of faith.

Personally, I have my own beliefs about healing, but choose not to instigate debate. Instead, I would like to travel the route of healing and answered prayer that has been an integral part of my life.

I remember the first time I experienced a healing from the Lord. Not that miracles hadn't already happened in the two years since becoming a Christian, but this one was a vivid example of God's character.

We gathered at a city park for our monthly outdoor church service. People stood and clapped and some watched from brightly colored blankets, sprawled on the meager grass. Summer had already claimed the little green there was in the dry, desert climate of Arizona.

I stood in the back of the large group of people, leaning on crutches to relieve the sharp pain in my right foot. I had a persistent heel spur that was going to be surgically removed that week. I hated the thought of an operation on my foot.

After worship music closed the service, people lined up for food: single moms with hoards of children, old men with backpacks in tow, teenagers whose appearance would bring scoffers to their toes in regular churches, and park dwellers mingling with the growing crowd.

I stayed behind and waited for the line to dwindle. A woman from church, dressed in her summer hat and wearing an apron, walked up to me and offered to pray for me.

"Can I pray for your foot?" she asked.

"Sure," I said, thinking she would just stand there and pray for me.

"No, I want to lay my hands on your feet," she gestured.

Being my silly self, I answered, "Great. And while you're down there, how about a massage?"

She knelt down, laid her hands on my feet, and began to pray quietly. Within a few minutes I felt a warm sensation go up my leg and a stinging pain in my foot.

Then I heard words spoken to me that weren't really audible—they seemed to be audible, but I can't explain how they sounded. I knew it was God.

"I will be your surgeon."

That was it. I placed my foot flat on the ground and began to walk without the crutches. My foot was fine; the pain was gone.

I looked around and wondered if anyone had noticed. It unnerved me to think of people watching and wondering if we were a traveling scam team out to make some money off a fake healing. But I really was healed.

Was it the lady who prayed for me, or a faith choice I made? I don't have definitive answers. I don't even want to try to figure it out or come up with a theory. All I know is at that time, in that park, God chose to heal me.

Sundays, when we were homebound because of my illness, John and I would attend virtual church. We could worship and listen to good teaching from a church locally or back on the East Coast—right in our living room. The Internet is a great resource when you can't get out. Many churches have live online services.

One morning while we were watching Pastor Lloyd Pulley of Calvary Chapel Old Bridge, New Jersey, he shared a quote from a woman who had used the text in her family newsletter. As I listened, I realized a physical healing isn't always God's priority. What we may think is good for us physically actually can hinder us spiritually.

I don't understand why sometimes there is a miraculous healing granted while other times there are unanswered prayers to healing. Sometimes God's no to our prayers can mean a yes to something greater in our heart. My question is this: What is more of a miracle—a healed body or a changed heart? Our bodies are just temporary, but our hearts and souls count for eternity. Changed hearts require our permission for the working of grace in our lives. God never forces us to change.[26]

Cindy has seen much suffering as she watches her husband, plagued by cancer, hold on and fight for his life.

A physical healing or a changed heart—which do you think will bring about more strength in a person? Which do you think will have lasting benefits?

One day I met a girlfriend at the grocery store. I was wheeling myself around with my broken leg (see chapter 8). We chatted for a while and she exclaimed her amazement that I had yet another physical hurdle to tackle. As many people have, she told me how much of an encouragement I always was for her.

But the story she shared next reminded me of the incredible care God has for us. Only a week before, Mindy had been hit by a train! And here she was proclaiming God's miraculous answer to prayer.

At her weekly Bible study, Mindy had shared how she felt like she always got along OK as a Christian, but never had seen the power of God really evident in her life. She wanted more. She wanted to experience God's sovereignty firsthand. So she had prayed that night for God to reveal Himself to her in a very real way.

The next day, she was on her way home with her two grandchildren in her vehicle. There was a railroad crossing before the turnoff to her house. As was customary when they came to this train crossing, Mindy had asked her granddaughter Ally, "Is there a train coming?"

"No, Grandma," Ally had chimed.

Mindy already had looked and did not see a train. She began to cross the tracks and out of nowhere, a train appeared a hundred feet from the crossing.

Mindy knew they would be hit if she didn't get off the tracks. Reacting with fear as the adrenaline shot through her body, she *thought* she floored the gas to take off, but instead found her vehicle in park. The train blew its horn as it passed in front of Mindy's eyes. The sight of her bumper flying down the tracks interrupted the blur of the cars from the train.

Ally had pleaded anxiously, "Grandma, back up."

Mindy put her vehicle in reverse as the train began to slow down. She turned to look at the kids and they were fine. They weren't even crying. She reassured them that God was in their car and they were going to be OK.

In reality, Mindy's vehicle should have been pushed along with the train and possibly smashed, injuring her and her two grandchildren. Instead, the train seared the front of her vehicle right down to the radiator. The car never budged. It remained in park, running—it was as if the train simply cut a slice off the front. This was physically impossible!

Mindy was fine, the kids were fine, and she stood there in shock thinking, *We just got hit by a train, and we are fine.*

After the accident, Mindy got a ride from a friend to pick up her other granddaughter, Sophie, from day care. Dazed at the moment, she clutched Sophie's take-home papers from her school basket and stuffed them in her purse. That evening, when everyone was gone, she was thinking about the day and wondering why God had saved them.

God showed Mindy: "I pulled Sophie's papers out of my purse to see what she had taken home and there was her week's memory verse; 'For by grace you have been saved through faith; and that not of yourselves, it is the gift of God' (Eph. 2:8 NASB).

"I cried and knew God had answered my request."

God had answered her prayer from the previous night. She asked Him to show her His power in her life. God knew this accident would happen and He not only saved them from disaster but also used this to display His love, care, protection, and compassion for Mindy. "For by grace you have been saved ..."

Prayer, persistence, and God's power—we pray for help, we are persistent in faith, and we must grab from God's power.

Isn't It Amazing?

From time to time there is a news story about a duck or a goose surviving and living with an arrow shot through its body. It's a strange story to hear—even more interesting is how often you hear it reported.

Here is one such story from the Yuma Daily Sun newspaper in Yuma, Arizona.

> A local veterinarian is treating the mallard duck that was swimming with an arrow protruding from its body and was rescued by the Yuma Fire Department from the canal near 1st Street and Avenue A.
>
> She said the arrow entered the duck above the right armpit and exited below the left armpit, puncturing her lungs and air sacs.
>
> "I haven't actually seen an arrow sticking out of a bird that is still alive, ever," Haugo said. "I thought, 'Oh my God,' but she is so darn lucky about this arrow... God was watching out for her."
>
> Haugo said the arrow "just missed the really important stuff," such as the heart and spine.
>
> She said the duck will not be able to return to the wild due to a fractured wing from the incident. "She will never be able to fly again."
>
> Currently, the duck is in rehab at Haugo's home, where she's had up to thirty ducks at one time. The recent addition makes a current total of five.
>
> It is unclear if she has any mortal injuries. For the most part, she is doing pretty good.[27]

This duck was persistent, but even the veterinarian had to give God the credit. How often do we encounter times in our lives where we feel we are going through each day with an arrow through our souls? Days when we want to fall away and stop the world around us from spinning with tornado strength?

Isn't it amazing what a prayer can do?

A few months after my first heart attack, my sister, Annie, was desperate to find help for me. She was convinced New York was where I needed to be after watching a morning news show about a cardiologist in New York City. Dr. Jeffrey Moses was heading up trials for medicated stents for Johnson & Johnson.

Like when I took the trip to San Diego, I was trying to be part of any trial with the new medicated stents. The ones placed in my vessels were constantly blocking back up. Dr. Canaday, my cardiologist, had to rotablade them to clean out build up. Each time he did this, the walls of my blood vessels became thinner, risking the chance of rupture and another heart attack.

My sister and I talked by phone one day.

"I'm going to call Dr. Moses and ask him to see you," Annie reaffirmed.

"You're crazy!" was my adamant reply. "He's famous. You won't get past the receptionist!"

After my sister hung up with me she placed her hand on her phone and prayed for the Lord to do a miracle and let her get through. Then she made the call.

"Dr. Jeffrey Moses' office," the receptionist answered.

"Can I speak to Dr. Moses?" my sister asked.

"Certainly, hold on a moment."

Dr. Moses picked up. Annie was amazed but she composed herself and explained my situation. He instructed her to have me send him my records and a CD with films from my last heart catheterization.

By August 26, 2002, I was in Lenox Hill Hospital in Manhattan where Dr. Moses performed a heart angioplasty on me. He not only placed two new stents in my vessels, but he was determined to clear the 100 percent blockage in my LAD—left anterior descending artery. This is the most important vessel and mine was completely blocked.

I remember waking up toward the end of the procedure. Dr. Moses was draped over my body, twisting the wire tubing that was threaded up to my heart. He was fiercely trying to clear the LAD. As he worked to free it, he yelled, "Come on, come on, let me at you!" His wiry hair was tossed back and his face was tense with determination.

Finally, the blockage was cleared and blood began to flow. Everyone in the operating room clapped.

While in recovery, I asked one of the nurses about his performance. She replied, "Oh, that's Dr. Moses. He's known as 'The Cowboy'!"

Nine months later, my main bypass (I had had a double-bypass open-heart surgery in February 2002) sustained a blockage right where it was connected to my LAD. If Dr. Moses had not cleared out the blockage, I certainly would have suffered a fatal heart attack. This was a prayer answered with many blessings attached!

Pray with expectation, not an agenda!

Earlier, when I was fighting for an opportunity to be part of the experimental surgery in Hershey, Pennsylvania, there were copious amounts of hurdles to overcome through the approval process before I was even accepted into the clinical trial.

My cardiologist at home was directed to perform all sorts of testing to be sure I met all the requirements for not only the efficacy of the drug, but also to be sure I would not suffer any undue complications from possible side effects.

Everyone in the medical community wanted me to have this opportunity; the evaluation was tempered with deep emotions and sighs of relief every time as I got past each requirement. A lot of prayer and many miracles happened on a regular basis. But once I traveled to Hershey, I had to go through another battery of tests before the actual surgery date.

Three days into the final testing at the Milton S. Hershey Medical Center, I received a sobering phone call at my hotel. Something in one of the requirements failed to match what had been done back home at my local doctor's office. I was going to be disqualified for the program.

I sunk into the ratty mattress in my shabby hotel room and let out a sigh of defeat. *Oh, Lord, please don't send me back home to die. Why would I get this far only to be turned down? Please, Lord, make it work out.*

I prayed silently to myself and then waited for the nurse to call me back with a final decision. I was preparing myself for the worst news.

Two hours later, my cell phone rang. The number on the display indicated it was from the hospital. I actually could see the building from my hotel window so I walked over to peer out in the distance as I spoke with the nurse.

"Well, we finished our evaluation and decided after all the testing was properly weighed, you will make the criteria for the clinical trial by the smallest margin. Be here tomorrow by nine A.M. for your surgery pre-op work-up. And by the way—congratulations!"

I was stunned. A few hours before I was facing defeat and possible death and now my life once more was presented to me as a token prize. How many times in a week or a day could I have life and death paraded before me?

Of course, the trial worked and played an enormous part in my being alive today.

Isn't it amazing?

From near-miss heart attacks, to experimental surgeries, I never knew what was going to happen to me when I awoke each day. I never knew what other miracle would keep me alive. One of the miracles that kept me alive was a small device on which I became very dependent.

By December 2002, pressure and problems with my heart were causing it to work hard to stay rhythmic. At one point, there were so many PVCs (premature ventricular contractions) that I needed to have an ablation to calm things down.

This is a procedure in which a specialized cardiologist called an "electrophysiological cardiologist"—who deals with abnormalities in the heart's electrical system—goes in through a catheterization and uses a laser to disengage the extra electrical pathways that are causing the heart to have abnormal heartbeats.

I was informed that the procedure could cause too much of the electrical system to be destroyed and leave me with a heartbeat that is too slow. If so, I would need a pacemaker implanted to keep my heart at the proper rate.

Of course, as things went for me, I woke up with a pacemaker implanted in my left shoulder. But I was happy to have gotten through the surgery and looked forward to once again trying to go home to rehabilitate.

Time went by and I became accustomed to the regular pacemaker checkups. I must admit, however, even though I had gained much compassion for elderly heart disease patients, I found it discouraging to sit in the waiting room for my pacemaker check with them. Although I often was told many young people also had heart disease hurdles, I always seemed to be the only young person in the waiting room.

One time I went in for my checkup and told the technician I was feeling *off*. My heart was staying at exactly 80 beats per minute, and I was often dizzy, weak, and, especially, worn-out.

Once the technician hooked me up to the diagnostic computer, she ran a few tests and asked me to wait until she returned with the doctor. My cardiologist came in after a few minutes and was surprised to see me sitting up.

"How do you feel?" he asked cautiously.

"Well, weak and funny," I answered. "What is going on?"

He answered me with a tone of disbelief. "Your pacemaker is now running at 100 percent. In other words, your heart has completely stopped beating on its own and is entirely dependent on the pacemaker. You are now 'pacemaker dependent' and your heart will never beat on its own again."

I was once again amazed at another miracle. If I had not needed an ablation and had a pacemaker implanted, my heart would have stopped beating and I would have been dead before I even landed on the ground.

"Pacemaker dependent" meant that the security check at the airport, a highly sensitive security sensor at a department store, or any other electromagnetic field could stop my pacemaker and kill me instantly. The news was leading me into a whole new way of living, but at least I was alive—again.

Prayer is answered every time we petition God for help. It may not be the way we intend or hope, but the answers from God are never the wrong ones.

In April 2005, one week before I had the near death experience in the ER, I was driving my son Jonathan to a doctor's appointment. He was fifteen and my husband already had let him drive our old truck in a field to get him accustomed to handling a vehicle larger than his dirt bike.

Jonathan sat up front, quiet and deep in thought. We were all tired of doctor's appointments. His was a routine checkup. *What was routine anyway?*

I drove along at sixty miles an hour, the radio playing to break up the awkward silence. Suddenly my face started to feel numb on one side as if I had been to the dentist and had a shot of Novocain. *Maybe my blood sugar levels are low and I need to eat something.*

But the numbness traveled down my side and both my legs became weak and jittery. I wanted to panic—to pull over and get help. But I looked at Jonathan and knew he needed me to be all right. *Am I having a stroke?*

I couldn't feel my feet and it seemed the gas and brake pedals had disappeared—like someone else was driving the van. I prayed, asking the Lord to help me get as far as the hospital. We were less than a mile away.

"Jonathan, how do you feel about driving?" He turned to look at me, not speaking a word.

My body quivered with tingling sensations. I held tight to the steering wheel and continued to pray we would make it without having an accident. I wasn't thinking about a heart attack. I wanted it to be OK for Jonathan.

We made it to the hospital and I was lucky to find a handicapped parking spot in front. When I pulled in and knew we were safe, I sat for a moment, hands still clutching the steering wheel.

I pulled the keys from the ignition, tossing them into my purse. When I stepped out onto the pavement, my knees buckled and I collapsed to the ground.

"Mom, are you OK?"

"Jonathan, you have to help me get to the ER. Go in the front entrance and ask the receptionist for a wheelchair. Tell her your mom needs to get to the ER. Hurry."

Jonathan ran across the parking lot and disappeared through the glass entry doors that closed automatically behind him.

I leaned against the van, trying to keep my composure.

Jonathan came back pushing a silver wheelchair, its blue vinyl backing painted with white lettering: "Hospital Property."

"The lady at the desk wanted my name and phone number. She thought I was going to steal the wheelchair. I tried to tell her you were having a heart attack and I had to get you to the ER."

Jonathan went from being in his mom's care to being the caretaker. I watched him speak with an air of confidence. He wasn't thwarted by the receptionist's distrust. He had a mission to save his mom. No one was going to stop him.

I clicked the lock for the van. Jonathan helped me into the wheelchair and we were off toward the entrance.

"Do you know how to get to the ER?" I asked Jonathan. The ER department was at the back of the hospital. I was so scared for him. He would have to weave his way through hallways and turns to find it.

"I know where it is, Mom."

ER nurses rushed out once we arrived and I looked back at Jonathan, who was taking a seat by himself on a chair. He was alone. I had a chance to phone my friend Terry to come pick him up. I hated to leave him there—he was only a kid.

Two hours later, I was being admitted to the hospital. Tachycardia, rapid heartbeats, had placed me close to a heart attack. It took a week in the hospital before I safely could return home.

It was a miracle I had been able to drive long enough to get us to the hospital safely and it was a miracle I hadn't had a heart attack right then, possibly causing an accident and hurting Jonathan and me or someone else.

Isn't it amazing!

I prayed and asked the Lord for healings. But each time one was answered, another life-threatening need would arise.

King David, in Psalm 6, wrote about deliverance from God while in deeply troubled times. In verse 2, he pleads for God to heal him: "Be merciful to me, LORD, for I am faint; O LORD, heal me, for my bones are in agony." And then in verse 9, David shows the answer from God after a cascading psalm of despair: "The LORD has heard my cry for mercy; the LORD accepts my prayer."

Jeremiah, in the Old Testament, makes a parallel statement: "Heal me, O LORD, and I shall be healed; save me, and I shall be saved: for thou art my praise" (Jer. 17:14 KJV).

As a young girl I remember looking for God to answer my prayer for healing. I developed diabetes when I was ten years old. It was traumatic for my mom, family, and me—thirty-eight years ago there was a lot less known about how to treat and live with diabetes.

At that time, my family was part of a traditional church in New York. Each Sunday one of the standard responses in the mass would be, "Only say the word, and I shall be healed" (see Matt. 8:8 NASB).

Every time I repeated this response, I would take a deep breath and wait for a moment, hoping God would heal me of diabetes. But the healing never came. Not truly knowing Jesus, I couldn't understand why He didn't heal me.

After becoming chronically ill with life-threatening heart disease, I found myself again pleading with the Lord for healing. But each time I prayed, I prayed with an agenda, wanting the healing to come in my own way and on my own timing.

It was like the day I cried out to God, "Lord, why haven't You healed me?"

His gentle reply was: "I cannot heal you until you are ready to accept how I choose to heal you. And I am not finished yet."

I still can feel the power of His response, and after He spoke those words to me I began to see all the ways He was answering prayer—maybe not by my design but definitely by His design.

Divine healing cannot be defined by *Webster's* dictionary nor can it be forced by our will. The answer for healing may not come until God's appointed time. Or the healing may be so different from what we prayed for that we might not recognize it as a healing. God's purpose for healing cannot be limited by our personal desires. The strength we gain by trusting Him to take us through our trials sets an example for others who may be suffering and in need of encouragement.

In his book *A Shepherd Looks at Psalm 23*, Phillip Keller uses his firsthand experience as a sheep rancher to take a unique look at this well-known psalm. He emphasizes the encouragement a Christian can be to others when he or she accepts the Shepherd's provision as they "walk through the valley of the shadow of death."

> It is a most reassuring and reinforcing experience to the child of God to discover that there is, even in the dark valley, a source of strength and courage to be found in God. Storms may break about me, predators may attack, the rivers of reverses may threaten to inundate me. But because He is in the situation with me, I shall not fear. The person with a powerful confidence in Christ; the one who has proved by past experience that God is with him in adversity; the one who walks through life's dark valleys without fear, his head held high, is the one who in turn is a tower of strength and a source of inspiration to his companions.[28]

Healing, or the process of getting well, comes when we realize God has a specific purpose for each of our lives. When we accept how He chooses to heal us, we then gain new strength not only for ourselves but also for those God puts in our path.

Throughout my years of illness, friends, acquaintances, and even perfect strangers have offered me, with sincerity, ways to get healed. And they still do as I continue to persevere through chronic illnesses. I know they are all looking out for me and have only the best intentions, but the offers always have a formula, whether it comes in a natural remedy, a product, a new discovery, a spiritual theory, or even a healer or place of healing to attend.

I recently met a sweet woman at a seminar. After laughing about my troublesome health issues, she began to tell me about a building that housed a healing center. She was positive that if I went there, God would heal me. I am sure there are some dynamic prayer warriors with this organization, but my reply shocked her and left her without a defensive answer. I used the wisdom from Cindy Mah, whom I quoted earlier in this chapter.

"I appreciate your concern, but what is more powerful—a physical healing or a changed heart? God is using me even in my weakness. I am sharing with so many people who are being encouraged by the absolute power of God in my life. If I were to be healed, I would be done. Oh, I would still have my story to tell, but by living it out each day, I can be a very real example of faithful perseverance."

She smiled at me and pondered my answer. I know some of the people who offer me solutions for my tragic health problems are wondering why I—or even they—pray anymore. Some people have come to a point of crisis in their view of prayer as I continue to reach more milestones of despairing health concerns rather than triumphant victories of powerful prayer.

In his seasoned wisdom, Australian Nick Vujicic illustrates his acceptance of God's will for his life. Nick was born without arms and legs, yet he now ministers to people all over the globe. Here is his idea of victorious living:

Circumstances do not have to change for you to become victorious. It is our hearts that need to be filled with the Holy Spirit.[29]

He writes this message on the front page of his website to encourage all people:

God has used me to let people know in countless schools, churches, prisons, orphanages, hospitals, stadiums, and in face-to-face encounters with individuals how very precious they are to God. Secondly, it's my pleasure to assure them that God does have a plan for their lives that is purposeful. For God took my life, one that others might disregard as having any significance, and filled me with His purpose and showed me His plans to move hearts and lives toward Him. Understanding this, though faced with struggles, you can overcome too.[30]

Why does it seem that we pray and yet sometimes, although we may believe God always answers our prayers, our requests fail to eventuate? I have found, through trial, study, and prayer, that prayer is not only to receive an answer. Here is a list of the main reasons we pray:

1. **God is close to us or near to us:** "What other nation is so great as to have their gods near them the way the LORD our God is near us whenever we pray to him?" (Deut. 4:7).

2. **God rewards us:** "And when you pray, you shall not be like the hypocrites. For they love to pray standing in the synagogues and on the corners of the streets, that they may be seen by men. Assuredly, I say to you, they have their reward. But you, when you pray, go into your room, and when you have shut your door, pray to your Father who is in the secret place; and your Father who sees in secret will reward you openly" (Matt. 6:5-6 NKJV).

3. **Not to fall into temptation:** "Then He said to them, 'My soul is exceedingly sorrowful, even to death. Stay here and watch with Me.' He went a little farther and fell on His face, and prayed, saying, 'O My Father, if it is possible, let this cup pass from Me; nevertheless, not as I will, but as You will.' Then He came to the disciples and found them sleeping, and said to Peter, 'What! Could you not watch with Me one hour? Watch and pray, lest you enter into temptation. The spirit indeed is willing, but the flesh is weak'" (Matt. 26:38-41 NKJV).

4. **God wants us to:** "But I say to you who hear: Love your enemies, do good to those who hate you, bless those who curse you, pray for those who mistreat you. If someone strikes you on one cheek, turn to him the other also. If someone takes your cloak, do not stop him from taking your tunic. Give to everyone who asks you, and if

anyone takes what belongs to you, do not demand it back. Do to others as you would have them do to you" (Luke 6:27-31).

5. **To be made well or healed:** "Is anyone among you suffering? Let him pray. Is anyone cheerful? Let him sing psalms. Is anyone among you sick? Let him call for the elders of the church, and let them pray over him, anointing him with oil in the name of the LORD. And the prayer of faith will save the sick, and the LORD will raise him up. And if he has committed sins, he will be forgiven. Confess your trespasses to one another, and pray for one another, that you may be healed. The effective, fervent prayer of a righteous man avails much. Elijah was a man with a nature like ours, and he prayed earnestly that it would not rain; and it did not rain on the land for three years and six months. And he prayed again, and the heaven gave rain, and the earth produced its fruit" (James 5:13-18 NKJV).

6. **So God can hear us:** "Then the priests, the Levites, arose and blessed the people, and their voice was heard; and their prayer came up to His holy dwelling place, to heaven" (2 Chron. 30:27 NKJV). "The LORD has heard my supplication; The LORD will receive my prayer" (Ps. 6:9 NKJV). "I call on you, O God, for you will answer me; give ear to me and hear my prayer" (Ps. 17:6).

7. **To please God; to make God happy:** "The LORD detests the sacrifice of the wicked, but the prayer of the upright pleases him" (Prov. 15:8).

8. **To receive an answer:** "Therefore I say to you, whatever things you ask when you pray, believe that you receive them, and you will have them" (Mark 11:24 NKJV).

9. **To receive peace from God:** "Be anxious for nothing, but in everything by prayer and supplication, with thanksgiving, let your requests be made known to God; and the peace of God, which surpasses all understanding, will guard your hearts and minds through Christ Jesus" (Phil. 4:6-7 NKJV).

Pray without an agenda. Pray without ceasing. Pray knowing God will answer in His own way, but for your own good. Then, when the miracles do come, don't doubt that God is the author. Too often a miracle comes from persistent prayer, and the petitioner does not accept the miracle for which he or she prayed.

Witnesses to a miracle either see God's power or deny what they know could not be physically possible. Consider the Israelites who had already witnessed many of God's miracles: "They refused to listen and failed to remember the miracles you performed among them… But you are a forgiving God, gracious and compassionate, slow to anger and abounding in love. Therefore you did not desert them" (Neh. 9:17). How easily they forgot and turned from Him!

What are miracles and what is their purpose? Bible scholar M.G. Easton says:

> Miracles are seals of a divine mission. The sacred writers appealed to them as proofs that they were messengers of God. Our Lord also appealed to miracles as a conclusive proof of his divine mission (John 5:20, 36; 10:25, 38). Where miracles are there certainly God is. Unbelievers deny that any testimony can prove a miracle, because they say miracles are impossible. An atheist or a pantheist must, as a matter of course, deny the possibility of miracles; but to one who believes in a personal God, who in His wisdom may see fit to interfere with the ordinary processes of nature, miracles are not impossible, nor are they incredible.[31]

Although atheists must deny the existence of miracles, like the Israelites who turned their backs on God, it is not that they can explain them away, just that they choose to ignore what they know to be true. The only time a miracle should be ignored is if it is counterfeit; that is, having at least two distinguishing characteristics. One test is if the miracle really is not supernatural in nature but merely a matter of slight of hand or some other sort of trickery or illusion. The other test is asking, "Does it lead you to Jesus? Does it come from God?" (see 2 Thess. 2).

Miracles also demonstrate God's bountiful love for people. David Wilkerson illustrates this point in his monthly newsletter:

As we search through the Gospel accounts, we're struck by the number of times Jesus performed miracles but instructed the people, "Do not tell anyone about this. Don't let this news be spread abroad." After healing two blind men, Christ told the men to keep the miracle to themselves. "Jesus straitly charged them, saying, See that no man know it" (Matt. 9:30 KJV). You see, Jesus didn't want the people following Him for His miracles. He wanted their devotion because His tender words captured their hearts.[32]

In the psalms, King David comes close to seeing God as being without mercy when so much tribulation comes upon him. "I cried out to God for help; I cried out to God to hear me. When I was in distress, I sought the LORD. ... Has God forgotten to be merciful? ... I will remember the deeds of the LORD; yes, I will remember your miracles of long ago. I will meditate on all your works and consider all your mighty deeds" (Ps. 77:1, 2, 9, 11, 12).

David stopped himself and took a look back at all God had done in his life. A miracle is the response of a yielded heart. A person's heart must also be surrendered to God to either perform a miracle or attest to one. David yielded his heart to God.

How many times has God performed miracles for us to see and know He is real, and yet in times of trouble we easily forget and fall into despair? No matter how many miracles we witness, it should only take one to build our faith. Where miracles occur, God is there!

Tim Hansel is the founder of Summit Expedition, a wilderness survival school for individuals seeking deeper experiences with themselves, others, and God. For years he has lived with continual physical pain, the result of a climbing mishap in the Sierras.

In his book *You Gotta Keep Dancin'*, Tim answers a question many people have asked over and over: "Why haven't you been healed?"

> For years, people have asked me, "Haven't you prayed to the Lord for healing?"
> My obvious answer: "Of course."
> "Why do you think He hasn't healed you?"
> "He has."
> "But I thought you were still in pain."

"I am."

"I don't understand."

"I have prayed hundreds, if not thousands, of times for the Lord to heal me—and he finally healed me of the need to be healed." I had discovered a peace inside the pain.[33]

Tim's revelation of healing comes from a heart so surrendered to God's will that he no longer needs to be healed in the way *Tim* desires. His healing is now in line with God's healing. That is where I find myself after all these years of pain and suffering.

Nancy Missler said something profound to me once: "He has wounded me in my life, but only in order to heal me."

Look for miracles and answered prayer not only in the actual answer you request, but in the perceived answer God knows is best for you.

CHAPTER 4

I Surrender All

All to Jesus I surrender; All to him I freely give.
I will ever love and trust Him,
In His presence daily live.
I surrender all. I surrender all. All to Thee,
my blessed Saviour,
I surrender all.[34]

THE WORDS *OPEN-HEART* surgery are not supposed to be comfortable words for anyone. But for me they brought an entirely new familiarity of surrender.

During open-heart surgery, the sternum—the breastbone holding the rib cage together—is sawed in half to open a patient's chest cavity to perform repairs on his or her heart. When the procedure is over, the surgeon pulls the rib cage back together and wires it up so it can heal.

The first open-heart surgery I had was plagued with complications. My sternum did not heal completely. Instead, it healed in two pieces with cartilage holding it together. The bone's movement caused me additional chest pain, adding confusion to my symptoms.

A heart surgeon, Dr. Nisco, who had assisted in my care, had to go in, clean out the scar tissue, re-cut the bone, and put my sternum back together so it could heal properly. It had been only a year since my original double-bypass open-heart surgery.

John and I met with Dr. Nisco to view the results of a CT scan. We followed him to an exam room and he closed the door behind us. He had a soft mannerism; his words and movements were always gentle and tender.

The room was dimly lit. Dr. Nisco flicked the light switch on the X-ray view box mounted on the pastel yellow wall. He glanced at the multiple pictures, pointing at each one with his pen.

"I don't see this very often. This rarely happens." He outlined the areas where the bone was separated and being held together by sparse areas of cartilage.

John and I stared at the images. I anticipated the news.

He turned to me as he shut off the light illuminating the X-ray film. "You know, some people have one major thing go wrong with their health. Some may have a couple of major health issues. But with you, everything turns out to be a major health issue." His genuine concern was evidence of his soft temperament and sympathy as he handed me the consent form for surgery.

People have asked me if I was scared when facing yet another surgery, encountering possible death from a heart attack, or experiencing complications of multiple heart procedures performed on me. My answer evolved over time. As with each setback, the feelings I experienced grew and developed into the completion I felt as I faced this unexpected surgery.

Surrender, when totally understood, reveals another dimension of freedom. I was wheeled into the pre-op room with a total peace. I shared jokes along with my faith, and smiles along with my grimaces from pain. I can say I actually believe that I finally reached completion of my surrender. To be so out of control and so free from anxiety comes when you have surrendered everything. God now has 100 percent of my life, my future, and me. Once I gave it all to Him, I no longer feared what could happen to me.

People tend to think that surrendering all is to give up all, but complete surrender brings enormous freedom.

I spoke with a friend a while back who was dealing with several heartbreaking trials. Her mom had been diagnosed with a fast-moving cancer; her niece, only days after being married, had to say goodbye to her new husband as he was deployed to Iraq; and another niece had a baby girl who was born with Down syndrome. She called me after her birthday and shared how she had retreated to her bedroom when her husband tried to surprise her with birthday festivities.

"I just didn't want to celebrate after all that was happening around me. I wanted to be alone, so I stayed in my bedroom and cried."

She told me after always giving so much, she now had reached a point where she could no longer give. Her only escape was to lock out everyone and take the time to cry and mourn. I truly believe that when we come to this point of brokenness, we must learn from our pain that all God wants is for us to surrender.

The word *surrender* is commonly understood as giving up possession of something into the power of another, or to relinquish control completely. It's usually thought of in a cowardly or feeble context.

In Nancy Missler's book *Private Worship, The Key to Joy*, she describes why surrender is necessary to grow closer to God:

Years ago, in one of David Wilkerson's newsletters, there was an article entitled, "The Making of a Man of God." I've never forgotten that intriguing title because, in a nutshell, this is what God is trying to do in all of our lives—make us men and women of God. If we really want to know how one becomes a "man of God," we have only to look at Jesus. This means that, at some point in our walk with the Lord, we too will experience rejection, confusion, and loneliness just as Jesus did. Each of these situations will provide us with a greater opportunity to die a little more to our self and to grow a little more in grace and the image of God.

John 12:24 validates this principle. Total surrender and relinquishment seem to be the cost of "becoming a man of God." Surrender Is Key: When God calls us to surrender all to Him, He is simply asking us to give back the life that He granted us in the first place. In other words, we're not being forced to lay our lives down; it's a choice that we are making out of our own free will and out of our love for Him.

When all is said and done, I truly believe we will not only be judged by what we did for Him, but by how much we surrendered to Him, how much we loved Him, and how much our hearts and lives were totally yielded to Him.[35]

A heart yielded to Him will exhibit a power we can draw only from the Lord. This power is a result of surrender and it is evident on the outside as well as the inside.

After an angioplasty, you have to lay flat for at least an hour or two to prevent bleeding from the femoral artery in your leg. A repair—an intervention—requires laying flat for up to eight hours.

Dr. Canaday did an angioplasty on my heart in his private heart cath lab. I named it "The Davenport"—after a cosmopolitan hotel in downtown Spokane, Washington—for its lavish décor, spacious patient rooms, and catered lunch service.

Warm, Sonora-colored tiles pave the lobby with resort caliber seating. A turquoise and teal glass sculpture hangs overhead, reflecting light from the cottage-style windows. Appointments are made with extra time for personal care, and nurses make sure every need is met to make your stay as pleasant as possible.

The Davenport, as I refer to it, is a nicely packaged version of the sterile operating rooms at the main hospital.

Unsure that I actually had a blockage, Dr. Canaday scheduled my heart cath in his lab to make things more convenient. If something were wrong, he would be unable to do repairs because of medical certification obstacles.

I woke up toward the end of the procedure to see the gray images of my heart reflecting from large monitors. I saw the familiar black outline of my main artery, and once again there was a narrow area where the silhouette thinned out, indicating another blockage.

A nurse packed gauze on the incision in my thigh and wheeled me over to the main hospital to have me admitted. Flat as an ironing board, I laid helpless under the skimpy, thin white sheet.

As we went through the glass covered bridge, connecting the Heart Institute to the hospital, I looked up at the sky through the clear dome overhead. Brilliant blue reflected down at me—a blue I wouldn't see for a while. The tunnel led me from one insensate building to another.

The hospital cath lab was booked until the next day. Once I got to a room, I was instructed to continue to lie flat until the next procedure. That would be another seventeen hours.

The heart cath was done the next morning and I was back in my room, staring up at the endless, dotted ceiling tiles.

Instructions were given, again, from the nurse. Each shift change, someone came in to be sure I followed the rules: no picking up or moving my right leg, no sitting up, no raising up my head, no getting out of bed—period.

Total time for my incarceration: thirty-six hours.

Jonathan called to offer me advice.

"Mom, concentrate on your left leg," he told me over the phone.

"What do you mean, Jonathan?" I was perplexed.

"Well, you can't move your right leg, but you can move your left leg a little so think about your left leg and move it as often as you want."

Not finding a reason to disagree, I took his advice. It did help to pass the time, even though I was limited in how much I could move my left leg. But at least I was able to move something!

My thirty-six hours ended right at eleven P.M. the next night. I was slowly allowed to sit up to be sure I didn't pass out. The freedom was refreshing and I walked the halls to get myself moving again.

The next morning, an aide came into my room. Betty was a shy, soft-natured woman who stopped by to speak with me often. She was a new Christian and liked to talk about her faith. I was sitting in front of the window, trying to absorb some of the warm sunshine and wondering what it would be like to smell fresh air.

"You look so peaceful sitting there with your brown, curly hair shining in the sunlight. It's almost like I am looking at Jesus," she commented. "I wish I had what you have." She knew what I had been through and was amazed at how happy and content I appeared.

"You do have what I have," I offered her. "You are a Christian who has asked Jesus to inhabit your heart and life. He gives all of us the same portion of faith, peace, and trust. We all have free access to His strength but it takes surrender of our will and desire to fight to let Him take over and handle all that we struggle with."

Betty stayed a bit and talked with me. I wanted her to know that Christian surrender is a powerful opposite to what the world knows surrender to be.

Kenneth W. Osbeck, in his book *Amazing Grace, 366 Inspiring Hymn Stories for Daily Devotions*, writes this about surrender based on the hymn "I Surrender All":

> The Bible teaches us that brokenness is a prerequisite to blessing and usefulness. No one ever achieves spiritual greatness until he has fully surrendered himself to God. Victorious living comes only as we abandon ourselves to the Lordship of Christ, becoming His loving bond slave. God's best for our lives is not the result of struggle. Rather, it is simply the acceptance of His perfect will and the recognition of His authority in every area of our lives.[36]

Victorious living is the result of painfully enduring a full surrendering of your self to God. You may look at people you know are suffering in many ways, and even your own suffering, and ask, "Where is this victorious living? I have suffered much pain and gone through many trials and still I cannot see any hope of victory. When will it come?"

It will come once you recognize what hinders peace and how to give all the offending problems to the Lord.

When I was two years into my illness, I felt I needed to talk to a Christian counselor—someone who was neutral and could help clear the way for my thoughts to be freed from some of the terrors that caused me to stumble. I found one and set up the first few appointments. One assignment he gave me that was supposed to last a week lasted only a half-day after I saw through its purpose.

He had instructed me to keep a sheet of paper for the week with two columns on it. One side would be a list of all the times I got depressed, angry, nervous, anxious, or mad. The other side would show whatever situation caused me the emotion. After writing down a few incidents, I understood his purpose—each situation that caused me grief was something I could not change. Each was a difficult issue that could not be avoided. There was nothing I could do. I had to let God take care of the things that rattled me. The way to do this was to surrender my trust, life, abilities, and entire being to God only.

Judson Van De Venter, author of "I Surrender All," wrote the following after surrendering his many talents to the Lord:

> For some time, I had struggled between developing my talents in the field of art and going into full-time evangelistic work. At last the pivotal hour of my life came, and I surrendered all. A new day was ushered into my life, I became an evangelist and discovered down deep in my soul a talent hitherto unknown to me. God had hidden a song in my heart, and touching a tender chord, He caused me to sing.[37]

When God knows you finally have surrendered all, you will also know because the victory that is meant for you will bring the freedom of complete joy.

As I hugged the shaken body of a grieving mom, shattered by the weight of a multitude of sorrows, I felt her despair.

"I am trying so hard to be strong for my kids," she sobbed, wiping the tears on her cheeks.

"You don't have to be strong. Surrender and let God be your strength. He can do it but we can't. We don't have to." I whispered the words in her ear, hoping to feel her tense, weighted shoulders ease into retreat, letting God bear the turmoil. But she couldn't let go, and I held onto her a little while more, desperate to share God's peace with her.

I reflected on the past few years of illness and tried to figure out how it was that I had obtained this peace. It is a peace that has freed me from trying to rely on my own strength. As I played back all the episodes of trials and tests dealt to me while I dodged heart attacks time and time again, I failed to find one specific event that pushed me through the door of surrender. I could see that it took day after day of physical pain and emotional agony to transform me into an empty vessel with only God left to save me.

I had no idea what God was doing in my life. I could not see the end of the goal. I knew nothing of God's purpose. All I had to do was let go and let God take me to the place He had for me.

The first time I rode a roller coaster, my body was riddled with fear from not knowing where I would end up or how tumultuous it would be getting there. The car slowly traveled up the squeaky, metal tracks, worn from years of repetitive rides delivering its occupants to the top of the high loop.

My hands desperately gripped the sides of the wooden seat as the ground below disappeared. Once at the summit, I looked out on the landscape. It was a grand view, laying out streets and neighborhoods far into the horizon.

After hanging on the top for an instant, the car careened down precipitous tracks, my eyes tearing from the fierce wind. I screamed all the way. It was like being in a freefall and wondering if the cord would hold me back from certain death. Once the cars slowed to a stop at the bottom, I realized how ridiculous it was to fear the end.

Now I choose not to ride a roller coaster. Nor would I try my luck at bungee jumping, hang gliding, or any other death-defying activity. But the way my life has changed since first getting sick is like riding that roller coaster—only not by choice.

What can I do? I'm at the top and the car must go down for the ride to continue and ultimately come to an end. Each trial I face is so different—it's like a whole new ride with more unknown twists and turns. There's no going back once the car is put into motion.

Life is that way. We are put into motion the day we are born. The ride will encounter sudden turns, hills to climb, unknown plunges over steep slopes, and surprises at every corner. How can people keep themselves in a state of peace and composure while the ride continues? How can people hold on when, for them, the next pitfall signifies imminent failure or destruction?

I became so wanting for my illness to end, or at least begin to end, that I prayed for God to take it away. My desperation sent me to an answer from the Lord that I had heard before. His answers always pointed the way back to Him—back to surrender.

I Surrender All

One Sunday morning in May 2003, God spoke to me in a quiet, calm voice and directed me to read Jeremiah 14:19-22. The words in brackets are what He instructed me to replace so I could make these verses a personal message:

Have You completely rejected Judah [me]? Or have You loathed Zion [me]? Why have You stricken us [me] so that we are [I am] beyond healing? We [I] waited for peace, but nothing good came; And for a time of healing, but behold, terror! We [I] know our [my] wickedness, O LORD, The iniquity of our fathers, for we [I] have sinned against You. Do not despise us, [me] for Your own name's sake; Do not disgrace the throne of Your glory; Remember and do not annul Your covenant with us. [me] Are there any among the idols of the nations who give rain? Or can the heavens grant showers? Is it not You, O LORD our [my] God? Therefore we [I] hope in You, for You are the one who has done all these things (NASB).

This was great praying on Jeremiah's part. Much like his kindred brother Job, Jeremiah acknowledges that only God can control much of the essentials in life. Only God can facilitate what happens each day we wake and live and work and play.

In her book *Out of Control and Loving it!,* Lisa Bevere talks about how God often "shakes us to wake us":

When God shakes us to wake us, we often find ourselves surrounded by the unfamiliar and unfriendly. God wakes us up from the secure by pushing us out of our comfort zone. By comfort zone I am referring to all that is familiar, expected, constant, and under our own control.

We are comfortable when what we expect happens. We enjoy being understood and supported by those around us. We prefer to have a constant source of financial provision. When God's flight training began in earnest in my life, I felt as if there was nothing to hold on to. It seemed my life was a sea of uncertainty. Everything that had been constant was in upheaval or transition. Our finances were lacking. Socially we were shunned. I felt alone, isolated, misunderstood, and persecuted. I prayed and cried out to the Lord for direction, only to hear my unanswered questions echoing back at me, I could find no rest. I was uncomfortable because I was experiencing God's shaking in every aspect of my life. His shaking removes what is temporary and leaves only what is of His kingdom. When God has shaken an area in your life, don't try to rebuild it yourself. Allow Him to restore only those things He wants to establish in your life.[38]

Being out of control *is* being surrendered. But as Lisa Bevere notes, God wants us to let Him restore and rebuild what we may lose in our relinquishing. And when we feel we have given more than our share or have surrendered all we can, there still may be some small parts of our lives we try to hold onto. We want to at least have something left in our control; some area that we feel God cannot shake or amputate. Yet to be totally out of control, to have nothing left, is truly a point where you can realize all you have is in God's power.

I once heard a quote by Mother Theresa: "You can't say Jesus is all you need until Jesus is all you've got." This amazing woman truly knew the reality of needing only God to live life. In her years of dedication to helping the dying and impoverished people of India, she understood the value of relying on God and Him alone.

Imagine the powerful effect we can have if we suffer enormous tragedy not only once or twice, but also through relentless, chronic suffering on a daily basis. If we choose bitterness, anger, and depression, our suffering is rendered powerless and inconsequential.

Yet if we choose to abdicate all our strife to God alone, and arise from the trials with joy and laughter, people around us will want to know, "How? How do you keep so upbeat in the face of tragedy?" We can then give an answer and point to total dependence on our God. Who benefits? We do, through strengthening our faith and the faith of those on whom we impress the power of prayer and surrender.

Sometimes surrender can bring us a more worthy gift than we can conceive.

My letter carrier was a sweet, dear lady who actually wrote me a note asking forgiveness when she inadvertently delivered someone else's mail to my house. I can hardly think of anyone as kind as she was.

But one day, her life began a shaking process that would turn everything upside down. Within one month, her husband announced he wanted a divorce; her only son, a successful financial advisor, was sent to prison for embezzlement; and she was diagnosed with amyotrophic lateral sclerosis (ALS), which is also known as Lou Gehrig's disease for the famed baseball player whose struggle with and death from this disease in 1941 brought it to national attention.

ALS is incurable. It's a progressive, degenerative neurological disorder. No one understands why it causes nerve cells of the brain and spinal cord that control voluntary muscle movement to gradually deteriorate. ALS leads to paralysis and death, usually in two to five years.

I couldn't imagine how much worse things could have gotten for her. Still, in her suffering she was out of control and surrendered to God. She was not concerned for herself but for others, as is evident by this letter she sent me:

Dear Cindy,

I have asked God to bless me with the right words to express what I need to say. Perhaps you have heard that I have been diagnosed with Lou Gehrig's Disease. I plan on taking different steps to fight the progression of this disease. However, the medical doctors don't give me any hope. You may already know that ALS is a disease that affects the nerves in your spinal cord, which sends pulses to your muscles. Eventually these neurons die and your muscles become more and more weak as time goes on. Anyway, to live in reality, should my efforts to stop the progression not work and God prefers to take me home to Him soon, I say soon because the doctors say two to five years, I would like you to know I believe it would please God, if I am a compatible match with you... I would like to do all of the tests and fill out the paperwork to make sure you get the use of my heart. I don't mean to give you any false hope. I do hope you will pray on this.

Love, your sister in Christ,
Shelia

Shelia wrote this letter on March 15, 2005. I can't express properly how her words made me feel. Here I was, complaining about my suffering and whining about being out of control. And here she was, willing to give me her *heart*.

I committed to pray for her to be healed. How could I even imagine her life for mine? I so wanted God to give back what she offered—complete surrender. I wanted her to be rewarded for her selflessness.

On September 25, 2005, six months later, I received an e-mail from one of Shelia's co-workers.

> Hello all,
> Remember Shelia that was diagnosed from two specialists that she had Lou Gehrig's disease and she had to quit work, and was not able to walk very good? Well, good news. Another doctor re-tested her for Lyme disease (symptoms are both quite the same) and she has that, in fact Acute Lyme disease. She will start antibiotic treatments and should be doing much, much better in a year or less. She had been tested four months ago for it, but the lab did not catch it. This last test was with a lab in California that specializes in Lyme disease. So does that make your day or what! I am doing the Happy Dance (not a pretty sight but I just can't help it).
> Becky

Shelia gave up her heart, and God gave it back to her with more love than it could ever hold before. These are the times the painful events in our lives allow us to see God's hand and power. "You have turned for me my mourning into dancing" (Ps. 30:11 NASB). Sometimes we dance with broken bones as David spoke of in Psalm 51:8: "The bones You have broken may rejoice" (NKJV). David, although a "man after God's own heart," knew the pain of brokenness.

David Swartz, in his book, *Dancing With Broken Bones*, describes King David's dilemma as not just a spiritual or physical brokenness, but also an opportunity for God to prove His love and care for us:

> For all of us, spiritual growth sometimes means going down a path we would much rather detour around. It means being broken into unstable pieces. But brokenness need not always hit with one great

big blow like as it did here in David's life. In fact, if we look closely, we will see incidents and relationships scattered across his life that should have reminded him regularly of his deep dependence on God. His spiritual bones were broken gradually.

But although David learned the hard way, he did learn. Christians everywhere sustain the same kinds of losses—but there is good news! No matter how broken we become, God can put all the pieces back together again. He alone can make us whole.[39]

A broken heart, a broken life, a broken relationship, and a broken promise—all these things can lead to a loss of hope. When your life breaks apart in front of you, the last thing you want to do is let go. Most of us would want to do whatever it takes to fix it.

Although we do need to live and do whatever we can, the root of our success is in our ability to lose control. Dependence on God is a good thing—not a weakness. Being broken is a pathway to growth—not defeat!

Years ago, I was driving through New York City. Stuck in traffic, I looked out onto the sidewalk, and slumped up against the cold, brick wall, was the figure of a man lying on the cruel, gray cement sidewalk. An empty wine bottle was clenched under his arm—testifying of his empty life. People walked over him, occasionally kicking his legs out of their way.

Is he alive? I wondered. I couldn't tell if he was breathing.

My car lunged forward as I grabbed a chance to move on. The dark figure weighed on my thoughts. I can picture him even now—a child of God, a living human being.

One moment in time and one small space in this huge city painted the core of bitterness and anger that seeped from every crevice. The intensity of its sharp taste burned as I reflected on what our world has become. I mulled over the distressing statements often heard from people struggling to get through their tattered lives:

"No one will ever tell me what to do."

"I run my own life. Where is God when you need him?"

"I can't even pray anymore—what's the use? Even the sight of a church turns me away."

"What type of a God would leave me here to suffer? Nothing will change. Nothing will ever get better. When I get to hell, I'll be ready. I've had lots of practice here."

The voices echo. People's pain covers the surface of their wounds like tightly bound gauze, oozing with burdens too difficult to bear. Bitterness has taken root. Can we as Christians become trapped by the same bitterness? Are we not susceptible to the anger that feeds its roots?

Many things can be attributed to the root of bitterness. Personal losses such as financial problems, housing, death of a family member or spouse, infertility, loss of employment, no transportation, poor health, and a loss of a sense of home by having to relocate all can cause bitterness. Then there are emotional losses—a friendship ends painfully, marital problems lead to divorce, children grow rebellious, and family members betray us.

The root of anger and bitterness often stems from—and feeds off—some kind of loss. Even as we strive to develop our relationship with the Lord, we can experience spiritual loss, which can be the most forbidding loss leading to bitterness.

> See to it that no one comes short of the grace of God; that no root of bitterness springing up causes trouble, and by it many be defiled.
> —Heb. 12:15 NASB

How do we destroy bitterness—root and all? In Job 38-42, he describes God's great works. When we look at what the Lord can do compared to our abilities, we see that only He can reach far enough to destroy the roots of bitterness so deeply embedded in our lives.

> Have you ever in your life commanded the morning, and caused the dawn to know its place? ... Have you entered into the springs of the sea, or walked in the recesses of the deep? ... Have you entered the storehouses of the snow, or have you seen the storehouses of the hail? ... Can you bind the chains of the Pleiades, or loose the cords of Orion? Can you lead forth a constellation in its season, and guide the Bear with her satellites? ... Can you lift up your voice to the clouds, so that

an abundance of water will cover you? Can you send forth lightnings that they may go and say to you, "Here we are"?

—Job 38:12, 16, 22, 31-32, 34-35 NASB

When I meet with people who are dismayed about their lives and the pain each day delivers, I try to share how my complete surrender sustains me because of God's power. Their response often is that they aren't like me and cannot give control to God as I have. They express defeat at what they feel is an impossible task.

Besides what I have to offer through my testimony, which continuously builds on surmounting trials, I share with them Paul's recollection of Abraham's faith when he stood on God's promises:

For what does the Scripture say? "ABRAHAM BELIEVED GOD, AND IT WAS CREDITED TO HIM AS RIGHTEOUSNESS." Without becoming weak in faith he contemplated his own body, now as good as dead since he was about a hundred years old, and the deadness of Sarah's womb; yet, with respect to the promise of God, he did not waver in unbelief but grew strong in faith, giving glory to God, and being fully assured that what God had promised, He was able also to perform. Therefore IT WAS ALSO CREDITED TO HIM AS RIGHTEOUSNESS (Rom. 4:3,19-22 NASB).

Nancy Missler wrote an insightful article about surrender:

Abandonment to God's will means a kind of weightless floating, having released all of our personal clutching for emotional and intellectual security, all of our personal needs to know and understand, all of our personal disturbances about being right, all of our personal humiliations at being wrong, making mistakes and looking stupid, and all of our personal frustrations over being denied what we thought God promised. It's being completely dead to all of our own "self" interests, passions, prejudices, pleasures and reputation and choosing, instead, to leave everything in God's hand.

Fenelon, the great sixteenth-century author and saint, expresses it this way: "Inward peace comes [only] with absolute surrender to the will of God. ... The reason you feel so agitated is that you do not accept everything that happens to you with complete trust in God. Put everything in His hand, and offer yourself to Him as a sacrifice. ... Until you reach a point of surrender, your life will be full of trouble and aggravation. ... So give your heart wholly to God and you will find peace and joy in the Holy Spirit."[40]

Choices come our way each day as we battle through life. Often the walls of despair become too high to see over.

When my son was little, we loved to visit the local corn maze in the fall. We enjoyed the crisp air, sweet robust apples, carved pumpkins, and the endless cornstalks that lined the opening to a corn maze acres deep. The fresh, pungent smell of alfalfa hay and harvested corn stalks rode the warm, soft breeze.

Without a map, children and parents were instructed where to start and where to exit the maze. "No breaking through the outside walls," the guide informed us.

One time Jonathan ran off with his friends and before I even had a sense of direction, he had gone through and exited the maze three times.

Trailing all the others, a friend and I became equally frustrated at the twisting turns and unfamiliar pathways. Finally, worn out and disenchanted, I broke through an outside wall, letting both of us out. I propped up as much of the corn as I could to cover up my folly.

Sometimes we only can look up past the high towering walls and plead with God to guide us through to the end. Breaking through a clouded wall of life's frustrations will not bring victory.

Since my illness, I have gained a new understanding of surrender. I have learned that surrendering all is something we have to determine to do every day. Knowing my life hangs loosely here on earth, I have learned to surrender my husband, my son, my family and friends, my goals and desires, and my life.

Yet when I think I truly have given all my ambitions over to God, another tragedy strikes, and I find I've taken back some of what I surrendered. Unlike sacrifice, which puts the attention on our efforts to please God, obedience hurts. Obedience requires us to tear off pieces of ourselves as we surrender all to the Lord. In Deuteronomy 4:4, the

Lord promises to keep safe those who cleave to Him: "But all of you who held fast to the Lord your God are still alive today."

Think of how many new beginnings God gives us each time we surrender something we have held so tightly. *Letting go* is *taking back* the life God wants us to live.

CHAPTER 5

One Is *Not* the Loneliest Number

'Cause one is the loneliest number that you'll ever do
One is the loneliest number, worse than two
One is the loneliest, number one is the loneliest
Number one is the loneliest number that you'll ever do[41]

THE MEAGER HOSPITAL room had a few radio stations available on the TV. The oldies station broadcasted this popular sixties song from Three Dog Night.

"Yes, one is the loneliest number," I complained under my breath. Sitting in the hospital for the umpteenth time, staring at the well-known, pale green walls, I remembered how a friend who also endured a heart transplant described the confinement. I asked her how she was doing after five long weeks of being isolated in her hospital room.

"You mean my box?" she replied.

Her description caused me to look about my room as the walls seemed to close in on me.

How I wished they were any other color besides sea-foam green. How I wished I wasn't so lonely and isolated. Depression slithered about, wrapping itself around each corner.

Loneliness is a word with far more meaning than we realize. Being lonely conjures up thoughts of one person, alone in a room, forgotten by everyone. But loneliness is often much more. At times, the feeling of being so isolated and separated from friends, family, the outside world, and sometimes even God drives us to an ultimate void. We can choose to drift deeper or we can choose to allow God's presence to saturate our days. I have been at this crossroad many times and sense I will visit this dilemma again and again.

During the hardest times of my battle with heart disease, I had lonely days in which I dragged my body from bed, weary at the thought of another day. I was tired and heavy with despair. My thoughts were of defeat and uselessness, wondering why I was even alive anymore. Many days I had a bottomless feeling that I had been forgotten. Sometimes long periods went by when no one called, no one came by to visit, and no one came to rescue me from the mundane routine of being home and alone.

It wasn't as though people didn't care to minister to me, but everyone had families, lives, and schedules. Being chronically ill or chronically anything gets old.

Being alone, feeling so isolated and separated from friends and the outside world, I began to feel my joy slipping away. Larry Crabb, in his book *Shattered Dreams,* talks of the despondency pain and trials can bring;

> Nothing makes me feel more alone than personal pain. When I'm in the middle of shattered dreams, I often hear myself saying, "If you knew the anguish I feel, if you knew how desperate I am despite how together I look, you would not taunt me with the promise of joy. You would come to me in my pain and just be with me, saying by your silent presence that my pain is justified and so too is my loss of hope. An invitation to dream higher dreams is as cruel as talking to a pilgrim lost in the burning desert about water that does not exist."[42]

One day, self-pity began to boil over until I had no room for any other thoughts. I wasn't reading my Bible or praying, and I eventually spiraled into a depression fringing on the side of anger.

I didn't want anyone to look at me. It was my privilege to be left alone.

This is the flavor of depression. Being so consumed with my own internal battles and external trials, I gave way to a pessimistic sense of inadequacy and total despondence. How does anyone return to the top of the hole dug by such a destructive state? I only had one choice left—use the solitude and lack of distractions to actually hear God, and God alone.

When I finally reached the end of all I had aspired to do, and when even my own voice was silenced, all distractions were gone and God's voice became intimate and close. Although alone, I could feel His presence wrapped around my feeble body.

Yes, there are medicines for depression, and chronic illness or emotional stresses may push a person's physiological state into a deficiency of certain chemicals in the brain. Medicines are sometimes needed. But the emotional and spiritual toll comes when we let go of the personal will to fight physically and the personal surrender to let God take control.

These feelings tend to be temporal examples and pose no real threat to a person's life. But depression can set in from loneliness and when it does, there is usually more than one cause.

Depression can come when deeper yearnings inside each person cry out for fulfillment. We desire friendship, companionship, comradeship— other people to share our experiences. There is also a tendency to seek a kinship in suffering—a misery-loves-company association. We want someone to understand our void and offer us some compassion or endowment that will replace our loneliness.

Many times during the years of hospital stays, doctor visits, lab appointments, a myriad of tests, and other appointments, I dreaded the shawl of loneliness that hung over my shoulders.

Friends, family, and my faithful husband were there for me countless times. Gifts, cards, dinners, financial help, and other acts of kindness were lavished on me. Sometimes a friend would drive me to an appointment and stay with me until I was done. Physically, I was not alone. But I often was emotionally lost into solitary suffering. *God, does anyone else have to go through this? When will it stop? When, God?*

Questions of despair clouded my thoughts and prevented me from seeing I was not really alone. God was—and is—always there for me. He is certainly bigger than the looming loneliness, keeping watch. He stays by my side and only wishes I would listen more to His communications.

Many people desperately want to hear God speaking. Our minds conjure up ideas of audible messages or direct dialogue with God. We wonder how God speaks. What language does He use?

Oswald Chambers, in his book *My Utmost for His Highest*, has a focused description of how God speaks to us:

> There is no escape when our Lord speaks. He always comes using His authority and taking hold of our understanding. Has the voice of God come to you directly? If it has, you cannot mistake the intimate insistence with which it has spoken to you. God speaks in the language you know best—not through your ears, but through your circumstances.[43]

"Through your circumstances" is a large ensemble of events, situations, and possibilities. I found many ways God spoke to me through my turmoil and pain once I was willing to see the more intricate ways He communicates.

C.S. Lewis, author and scholar, agrees:

> God whispers to us in our pleasures, speaks in our conscience, but shouts in our pains: it is His megaphone to rouse a deaf world.[44]

In what other specific ways does a God who is infinite in wisdom, omnipresent, and creator of all things speak to us?

Through His Word

Sitting in church before the service one Sunday morning, I pondered yet another heart procedure that was scheduled for the next day. Testing showed a massive blockage in my heart's main artery. In a quiet whisper, I was led to open my Bible to Jeremiah 33:6. *Oh, what now, Lord, another inspirational verse?* I was cynical and unreceptive. But I read (what is in the brackets is what the Lord told me to substitute to make it personal):

Behold, I will bring it [you] health and cure, and I will cure them [you], and will reveal unto them [you] the abundance of peace and truth.

—KJV

That next day the procedure was done—but no blockage was found. God healed me as He had spoken to me through His Word.

Through Speaking to Us in Our Minds

In December 2001, only three months after first developing heart disease, I was praying for God to heal me. His reply, which I heard in my mind, was less then encouraging: "I cannot heal you until you are ready to accept how I choose to heal you—and I am not finished yet!"

OK, I thought, *I will wait for You to be finished.*

How pompous I must have sounded to the Lord. Instead of a sweet-smelling aroma rising to Him in the heavens, I was like a noisome complainer!

What I could not comprehend was that His promise of healing would not take on *my* design and resolution, but *His* will and desire. His timing and His ways often do not make any sense to our minds.

What seemed to be an answer with an ending—"I am not finished yet"—actually was an admonition for me to continue listening to Him and finding my source of endurance only through Him.

Though I did not then realize the power of His words, I know now that His promise has been fulfilled over and over, and I take comfort in His care.

Through His Creation in Nature

The day I came home from the hospital in the summer of 2005, after having died and been brought back twice, I sat on a chair in my backyard. The sun's warmth soothed me and I prayed quietly, asking the Lord if He would allow me to live much longer.

Suddenly, I heard a hawk's call and looked up to the sky. Three hawks were circling above me—not a common sight in my suburban neighborhood. I thought of the Trinity and took solace.

"You will fly free like the hawks above," the Lord spoke to me.

A week later, I stepped out my front door and found a long hawk feather from a large hawk. What are the odds of one of those hawks losing a feather in the right spot with the right wind to cause it to land on my front porch?

Another week later, on the way home from church, three hawks swooped down over our van as my husband drove home. They almost crashed into our windshield. Again the Lord whispered to me, "You will fly free like the hawks above."

A few weeks later I received a miracle heart transplant! If I had not received that heart transplant, I surely would have died.

Through Physical Items

On one particularly tough day I sat despondent, staring out the window. I watched as the letter carrier delivered the mail to our mailbox.

"Go out and get the mail," the Lord prompted me—a task not done easily for me. I was so bad off that walking to the mailbox was almost impossible. But I trudged down the steps and got the mail.

By the time I got back to the house, I was so short of breath I collapsed on the couch.

In the pile were two greeting cards—one from a dear friend, the other from an anonymous sender. Both were postmarked the same day, from different states, and in different colored envelopes. But they were the exact same card! What was the verse on the front?

> I will lift up my eyes to the hills—where does my help come from?
> My help comes from the Lord, the Maker of heaven and earth.
> —Ps. 121:1-2

That verse was exactly what I needed to hear. Receiving those two cards on the same day was like receiving a personal letter from God!

Through His Chastening

Coming home from a doctor's appointment one day, sobbing uncontrollably, I begged the Lord to speak to me and tell me what to do. The doctor I had at the time, like many previous ones I had seen for my heart condition, was callous and intent on blaming my symptoms on psychiatric problems.

The Lord instantly put an idea in my head to call a girlfriend. *Why, Lord? She doesn't know anything about heart disease!*

Stubbornly, I opposed the Lord's prompting until I finally called her. She told me she had a friend whose husband is a cardiologist and a Christian! The end result was finding the doctor I still see today. He not only is a gem, but he has saved my life countless times.

Through Uncertainty

Waiting one evening at the hospital to have an emergency heart procedure, I became frustrated as one emergency after another came and went and my own procedure was delayed several times. After seven hours of waiting, I finally asked the Lord to allow His will and give me a peace about the outcome. *Should I go through with this, Lord?*

Soon after I prayed, a nurse came into my room and informed me the procedure had to be cancelled. Instead of being angry, I was relieved. That next day the doctors figured out something else was wrong and the problem was treated easily with medication.

When we feel the most alone and even distant from God, He is still there, just as close as He always was and is. When we feel there is nothing left to our existence, God's presence can saturate our days. Truly being void of all our support systems opens up the entrance for the power of God's infinite presence. Whatever your trial, no matter what burden suppresses your desire to go on living, you truly are not alone.

After those memorable lines from Three Dog Night chimed from the radio, I realized it wasn't true. I knew that even as God exists, there is never a time that any person on this vast earth is ever really alone.

Another unforgettable song exemplifies the way God speaks to our inner soul during times of distress. Written by Elizabeth P. Prentiss, "More Love to Thee" is a hymn inspired by a lifetime of great suffering.

Mrs. Elizabeth Payson Prentiss, born in Portland, Maine, on October 26, 1818, was known throughout her life as a saintly woman, who continually practiced the presence of Christ. Those who knew her best described her as "a very, bright-eyed, little woman, with a keen sense of humor, who cared more to shine in her own happy household than in a wide circle of society." Though Elizabeth was strong in spirit, she was frail in body. Throughout her life she was a near invalid, scarcely knowing a moment free of pain. She once wrote these words:

"I see now that to live for God, whether one is allowed ability to be actively useful or not, is a great thing, and that it is a wonderful mercy to be allowed even to suffer, if thereby one can glorify Him."

"More Love to Thee" was written during a time of great personal sorrow. While ministering to a church in New York City during the 1850s, the Prentisses lost a child, and then a short time later their youngest child also died. For weeks, Elizabeth was inconsolable, and in her diary she wrote, "Empty hands, a worn-out, exhausted body, and unutterable longings to flee from a world that has so many sharp experiences."

During this period of grief, Mrs. Prentiss began meditating upon the story of Jacob in the Old Testament, and how God met him in a very special way during his moments of sorrow and deepest need. She prayed earnestly that she too might have a similar experience.[45]

Her prayer for this personal knowledge inspired a poem. It was first printed as a leaflet in 1869 and later published in the hymnal *Songs of Devotion*. "More Love to Thee" is translated in many languages and still touches many with the message of sorrow and love.

More love to Thee, O Christ, More love to Thee!
Hear Thou the prayer I make on bended knee.
This is my earnest plea: More love, O Christ, to Thee;
More love to Thee, More love to Thee!

Once earthly joy I craved, Sought peace and rest;
Now Thee alone I seek; Give what is best.
This all my prayer shall be: More love,
O Christ to Thee;
More love to Thee, More love to Thee!

Let sorrow do its work, come grief or pain;
Sweet are Thy messengers, sweet their refrain,
When they can sing with me: More love,
O Christ, to Thee;
More love to Thee, More love to Thee!

When we read prose like this and we experience isolation caused by any kind of circumstance in our lives, we can choose to follow and love God as Mrs. Prentiss did.

Not only do we love God, but also resting in His love removes the fears that come with painful times. As Nancy Missler says:

The reason it's so important to know God's love is because when we see His handprint of love in every aspect of our lives, we'll never fear what He might allow into our lives.[46]

How can we possibly tune in to these ways God speaks to us once we realize how He speaks?

One such story of revelation is found in the Old Testament book of Genesis. The story of an Egyptian slave, Hagar, and her unhappy plight ultimately led to an encounter with an angel of God that marked a theological commencement for the people of her day.

Hagar means "fugitive, immigrant, or stranger," and those things she was as an Egyptian woman in a life of slavery. Hagar was cut off from her home and identity as she was forced to become Sarah's handmaid (Abraham's wife).

Hagar was considered a concubine—a woman who co-habits with a man or functions as a second wife without the legal standing of a full wife. Sarah gave Hagar to Abraham to acquire a child through Hagar for herself (see Gen. 16:2).

Sarah made life hard for Hagar. Sarah wanted to bear Abraham a child. As she grew older and older, she became desperate. Although Sarah gave Hagar to Abraham to bear a child for them, she held contempt for the woman who would fulfill her husband's desire. Genesis 16:6-10, 13-14, gives a detailed account of Hagar's angelic visitation:

> So Sarai treated her harshly, and she fled from her presence. Now the angel of the LORD found her by a spring of water in the wilderness, by the spring on the way to Shur. He said, "Hagar, Sarai's maid, where have you come from and where are you going?" And she said, "I am fleeing from the presence of my mistress Sarai." Then the angel of the LORD said to her, "Return to your mistress, and submit yourself to her authority." Moreover, the angel of the LORD said to her, "I will greatly multiply your descendants so that they will be too many to count." Then she called the name of the LORD who spoke to her, "You are a God who sees"; for she said, "Have I even remained alive here after seeing Him?" Therefore the well was called Beer-lahai-roi; behold, it is between Kadesh and Bered."
>
> —NASB

Hagar recognized a deity had spoken to her. She then called God, "El Roi, You are the God who sees me," and she named the well where she met God "Beer Lahi Roi," or "well of the Living One who sees me."

In her book *Lost Women of the Bible*, Carolyn Custis James discusses this time in Hagar's life when she overcame loneliness with her new, intimate relationship to God:

> In her encounter with the angel of God, Hagar received dignity and meaning. The simple but unchanging truth that God's eyes were fixed on her empowered her with a kind of freedom no one could ever take away. She was not alone. She *did* matter.
>
> No one else in Scripture—male or female—ever names God. Hagar does. The new name she gives to God expresses her most basic theological conviction: she is not invisible to God.[47]

Hagar was an Egyptian slave woman—yet God met her where she was. He called her by her name. She had no previous knowledge of God, she was pregnant with a rebel child, and she was a woman.

We think God cannot speak to us if we are turned away from Him, not living up to certain standards as a Christian, or living in some kind of sin or rebellion. What do you feel keeps God from speaking to you? He is always speaking to you. You just have to listen!

Carolyn Custis James finishes her story about Hagar with this sage advice:

It just goes to show how lonely life can be amid the hustle and bustle of activities, errands, crowds, and friendships. Even inside a good marriage or close friendship, there's still a dimension of isolation we cannot escape. For all of us, there are plenty of wilderness experiences when we suffer symptoms of isolation and insignificance. For all of us, there are inevitable moments when, even surrounded by loving family and friends, we feel invisible or go through something alone. A surgery, divorce, a death, a failure. Those sleepless nights, those closet moments, those tears we shed in private. What we wouldn't give to find Hagar's spring and to be found by the Angel of the Lord.[48]

It is in the hardest times in life that God lets us know He is a God who sees us.

How much did I still have to suffer through? Questions like that place my eyes on my situation. We can get so caught up in our pain and suffering that we can't hear God speaking to us. As Nancy Missler said, "The reason it's so important to know God's love is because when we see His handprint of love in every aspect of our lives, we'll never fear what He might allow into our lives."

We have to realize God loves us. Whatever is happening, He is a God who sees us! And He speaks to us in so many ways.

Larry Crabb stresses the ability to see past our shattered dreams, pain and loneliness:

The dream to experience God rises from deep within me. I see the possibility of living beyond shattered dreams.[49]

Lonely? Love God. Let Him in so He can dissipate the loneliness crippling you. One is *not* the loneliest number!

CHAPTER 6

Ya Gotta Laugh

WHY A CHAPTER about laughing? Since 2001, my life no longer rests in the category of "normal." Trials I hoped would not happen until I already had lived many long years of happiness, health, and vibrancy have now propelled me into the future. Brittle bones, memory loss, swollen feet and legs, fatigue, and many other symptoms constantly plague me. These maladies make me try even harder to find ways to combat the assault.

Laughter is one of my defenses.

The word laugh, according to the *American Heritage Dictionary*, means, "To express certain emotions, especially mirth or delight; to show or feel amusement or good humor; to feel a triumphant or exultant sense of well-being."[50]

Merriam-Webster's Dictionary also describes laughter as "to be of a kind that inspires joy."[51]

The word *silly* (as I think of myself) in the Greek is *selig*, which means blessed, happy, or blissful.

My hope is to make you laugh and to inspire you with joy—"the joy of the Lord." Remember, one of my anchor verses is "The joy of the LORD is your strength" (Neh. 8:10 NASB).

Laughter is also good medicine. What happens when we laugh? We change physiologically. We stretch muscles throughout our face and body, our pulse and blood pressure go up, and we breathe faster, sending more oxygen to our tissues. And laughter appears to burn calories too. Maciej Buchowski, a researcher from Vanderbilt University in Nashville, Tennessee, conducted a small study in which he measured the amount of calories burned in laughing. It turned out that ten to fifteen minutes of laughter burned fifty calories.

There are other health benefits of humor and laughter:

Laughter activates the chemistry of the will to live and increases our capacity to fight disease. Laughing relaxes the body and reduces problems associated with high blood pressure, strokes, arthritis, and ulcers. Some research suggests that laughter may also reduce the risk of heart disease. Historically, research has shown that distressing emotions (depression, anger, anxiety, and stress) are all related to heart disease. A study done at the University of Maryland Medical Center suggests that a good sense of humor and the ability to laugh at stressful situations helps mitigate the damaging physical effects of distressing emotions.[52]

A good hearty laugh can help reduce stress, lower blood pressure, elevate mood, boost the immune system, improve brain functioning, protect the heart, connect you to others, foster instant relaxation, and make you feel good. Laughter decreases stress hormones and increases infection-fighting antibodies. It increases our attentiveness, heart rate, and pulse.[53]

Why wouldn't you want to have a good laugh? Here's what God's Word says about laughter:

A merry heart doeth good like a medicine.
—Prov. 17:22 KJV

Then was our mouth filled with laughter, and our tongue with singing: then said they among the heathen, The LORD hath done great things for them.
—Ps. 126:2 KJV

In Tim Hansel's book *You Gotta Keep Dancin'*, laughter is hailed as paramount for making life fun. He taught a special class at Azusa Pacific University with optimum health as its focus:

> Tre was in our class. Some serious congenital problems had left her with only one leg that could do no more than hold a shoe. She had a total of six stubby fingers. But if you were to meet her, you most likely would agree with the class [they unanimously had chosen Tre Bernhard as the greatest living example of wholeness they ever had known] because the two most predominant features about Tre are her incredible compassion and her lively sense of humor. Tre had been through hardships even worse than her physical handicaps. She had lived a life that would devastate most people, yet she chose to transcend the situation and give the world a tangible sense of love and humor that changed more than one life, including my own.
>
> Humor has the unshakable ability to break life up into little pieces and make it livable. Laughter adds richness, texture, and color to otherwise ordinary days. It is a gift, choice, a discipline, and an art.[54]

Laughter comes from a heart filled with God's love. If you can't seem to get a good laugh going, then let me help you out.

The next few stories are true—I did not embellish them for this writing. They may not be in the order they happened, but real they are! My friends no longer say Murphy's Law—they say it's Cindy's Law!

Go ahead, have a good laugh on me!

I have some one-liners most people find quite amusing. How about my reasons for still being alive?

"It's too hard for them to kill me off. I'm from New York—we don't die easy!"

"I keep trying to get to heaven before everyone else, but I keep missing!"

When I finally got out of a wheelchair and onto crutches after breaking my leg, it felt good to stand—even if it was with crutches. I am only five-two, but my remark was exasperated: "I feel so tall!"

Sometimes doctor visits can be amusing. One doctor in Seattle was quite the sarcastic one. When I told him how people tell me I look great for what I have been through, his reply was, "You don't look so great to me!"

I explained I had seen seven other cardiologists before him. He asked, "What happened to them?"

I wanted to give him some of his own medicine, so my reply was, "Oh, they are floating down the Spokane River by now." That stopped him from getting the last word!

Sometimes nurses at doctor's offices can be quite surly after a long day. During one of my appointments after my heart transplant, I was complaining about my weight gain. The nurse's reply was, "At least you don't wiggle when you walk." I guess she considered me "fat but firm."

That same nurse, and I do love her, had a great idea when I broke my leg. Being on crutches made it hard to get around, and often I had to explain that I hadn't broken it skiing or snowboarding. (I live in the snow country of Washington state, so that is a logical assumption when someone is on crutches in the winter.)

Her idea was almost as good as mine: "Just tell people you had a heart transplant and now you are looking for a new leg!"

OK, I thought that was cute. Mine is a bit more of a chuckle-buster: "No, I didn't break my leg skiing. I was stealing coconuts in Florida!" (You can read about my mishap in chapter 8.)

She also referred to my unimaginable bad luck as being reminiscent of the story line in the film *Planes, Trains, and Automobiles* when the plot follows the story of character Neal Page as he tries to return to his family in Chicago for Thanksgiving after a business trip in New York. The journey is doomed from the outset with everything possible going wrong.

Hey, at least we can laugh!

There have also been attempts on my part to "work the system," as you might say.

After being on a pacemaker for almost six months, I noticed one day that I felt more lethargic than usual. My heart rate was a steady eighty beats per minute. I checked it several times throughout the day and it was always eighty beats per minute.

After a few days like this, I went in to see my cardiologist and a technician tested my pacemaker.

Everything was fine with the pacemaker, but the reason for the constant eighty beats per minute was my heart was no longer beating on its own. The pacemaker had taken over entirely.

I thought about that and then asked my cardiologist to make out a death certificate.

"What for?" he asked in shock.

My reply was not what he expected. "Well, if my heart is no longer beating on its own, then I am actually dead! If you make out a death certificate, I can send it in to my life insurance company and collect my life insurance. I could really use the money now!"

Of course, I couldn't seem to convince him!

When I had to prepare for my trip to Hershey, Pennsylvania, where I was taking part in the experimental surgery that grew new arteries around my heart, I knew my husband, son, and I were facing five weeks in a hotel.

Looking for the most economical housing, I called the Ronald McDonald House in Hershey. They told me only sick children and their families were able to use their facilities. My line to a newspaper reporter, which she found comical enough to use in her article about my surgery, was, "I tried to get into the Ronald McDonald House, but I was too tall!"

Speaking of accommodations, in August 2002 when I traveled with my husband to New York City to have a procedure, we had to find a hotel in Manhattan for one night. The cardiologist performing the heart catheterization did not want me to travel the same day I was discharged.

My husband tried to find a room close to the hospital, but the area of Manhattan by the hospital was affluent and rooms were expensive. One night in a basic accommodation was no less then five hundred dollars a night.

So he visited Hotels.com to see what he could find. He got us a room for eighty-nine dollars only a few blocks from the hospital.

"How did you find that deal?" I asked him as we hailed a cab.

"Oh, it was one of those specials. But at least it's close by."

We traveled the few blocks by cab so I wouldn't have to walk far. We were dropped off in front of the hotel, its name palely displayed on an old building: "The Habitat."

"The Habitat?" I questioned. "Is that like a hostel for traveling students?"

John was quiet as we entered the doors.

Inside we stared as employees clad in black pants and shirts waited on clients. The lobby was surreal with a mixture of modern décor and dark furnishings. To the left of the front entrance was a dance club with a disco mirror ball glaring down on dark bodies dancing to primal music.

"This is where we are staying?" I asked.

"There's nothing else around here," John replied.

We checked in and walked up a flight of stairs to an old cage-like elevator, then we traveled slowly up to the sixth floor where our room was. Dingy, stained walls surrounded dark hallways as we found our room number. After opening the door and stepping in, we realized why it was so cheap.

The room was only as wide as it was deep, maybe seven feet by nine feet. An aged air conditioner leaned dangerously on the ledge of an old window. At least we would have cool air. I noticed a freestanding sink next to a small, worn-out television.

"Where is the actual bathroom?" I remarked. John walked down the hall and found two bathrooms—or, should I say, toilet closets. Each was the size of an actual closet with only a toilet sitting in the middle and a light bulb in the ceiling.

"I won't use these bathrooms tonight without you guarding the door!" I nervously stated.

Next we had to find a shower—any shower. So we continued down the hallway and found a community bathing room. Looking in at the tattered walls and filthy shower stalls, we decided a shower could wait until we left the next day and returned to family where we were staying.

Back to the room: I noticed there was only one twin-sized bed! John pulled it away from the wall and found that the top mattress slid out to reveal another mattress underneath. When it was fully open, it made a double bed with two mattresses. But once the bed was opened far enough for us to both sleep on it, we no longer could open the door!

"Oh, this is great," I moaned. "I can see me now having to go the bathroom tonight. I'll have to roll over you to get out of the bed, have you get up and fold up the bed, walk down the hallway hoping we don't get mugged, and then manage to use the 'toilet closet' without totally freaking out!"

We decided to make the best of it. We opened the bed, locked the door, and settled in to watch some television.

After falling asleep, like clockwork, I woke up around two A.M. to go to the bathroom. I woke up John; we rolled out of the bed, slid the top mattress back against the wall, and walked down the hallway to the toilet closets. I made sure John stayed posted outside my door.

But when I was done and opened the door, he was not there. My poor heart, just being poked and prodded, started to race.

"John, where are you!" I whispered as boldly as I dared.

For a scary moment, I thought he had been mugged or that I would find him down the dark hallway, murdered by an intruder.

As soon as I called out to him, he appeared, emerging from the toilet closet next to me. "What's wrong?" he chided me. "I had to use the bathroom too."

We went back to the room and the night passed with no more interruptions. I was one happy person when we checked out the next day! Don't ya love New York?

There have been other unforeseen hazards relating to my many appointments and checkups.

One time I was lying on an exam table having a bone density test. As it was finished, the technician tried to retract the top of it so I could sit up and get off the table. Each time she tried to retract it, it made a grinding noise and moved only an inch or so. She tried and tried, and after ten or fifteen minutes, I suggested she let me crawl out of the machine.

"Oh, no," she said. "That won't be OK. I don't know what is wrong. This has never happened before." She kept trying.

"Look, I am not really old with brittle bones. I can safely crawl out of this if you would let me." I definitely wanted to get out of that machine.

She finally agreed and I crawled out. As I left, I could still hear the machine grinding away as she tried to unlock it.

I have multiple visits to the lab for blood work. Sometimes I go so often I see the same lab personnel more than once in the same week. Within six months, the centrifugal machine that spins the blood sample to separate it for testing blew up two times while they were spinning my blood.

Blew up! Gone. The expensive machine was totally broken and had to be replaced. This can happen at times, but to happen twice within six months with *my* blood in it made the lab technicians pay attention. I wonder how they feel now when I walk in for my monthly blood work.

I've had many embarrassing moments too. I was leaving a grocery store after having a pacemaker put in to keep my heart beating properly. I had a large cart of groceries and was going through the security screens when the alarm went off. A young store clerk came over to check my cart. He looked and looked but couldn't find anything with a security tag on it. Finally I told him I had a pacemaker. He felt silly and walked away quietly. I, of course, felt just as silly that I was so young looking he never thought of my having a pacemaker!

I've met some pretty special people since getting sick. One such person, Melinda, has gone through as much as—if not more—than I have. We used to get together and whine about our situations, but sometimes the whining gave way to creative laughter.

Before my transplant, while I was still able to drive, Melinda called and asked if I could take her to her heart catheterization—part of the yearly checkup a transplant patient must go through to keep tabs on his or her new heart. She was scheduled for early in the morning—very early, but I knew she needed someone not only to drive her, but also to be with her.

The day before, I had my pacemaker adjusted. My sleeping heart was totally dependent on the device for the electrical impulses it needed to keep beating. Most of the time I was tired from all the medications, machines, and appointments I faced. Four A.M. would be early! But she needed to be at the hospital by five A.M.

I woke up to my alarm that Thursday with a groggy murmur. When I got to Melinda's, she was waiting at the door. We got in my van and headed out. While driving on the highway to the hospital, I had a disconcerting idea.

"You know, if one of us has a heart attack, the other will have a heart attack from the emotional stress. So who will call 911? Look at us—it's the blind leading the blind!"

We laughed all the rest of the way to the hospital!

I know I have mentioned having been an inpatient at my local hospital more than fifty-five times. So I had many opportunities to experience everyday hospital mishaps. Of course, someone visiting a few times over many years never may fall into some of the silly things that happen, but with my frequent visits, you know things are going to go awry.

Early on in my heart catheterization "career" I learned about the aftermath of such a procedure. Lying flat afterward became frequent and routine—most of the time.

After one procedure, when I was granted privileges to vacate my hospital bed, I ran for the bathroom, locked myself in, and wouldn't come out for an hour. I did not want to see another bedpan and I wanted the freedom to say, "Stay away from me!"

OK, my first heart cath was traumatic with the doctors trying to avoid open-heart surgery or death. I don't even remember how long I had to lie flat then. But consider this: lying flat after this procedure means (and you may have been here already) FLAT. No moving any body part except for your arms. No moving your legs, unless you have permission to wiggle the opposite leg a bit. No moving your torso. And absolutely *no* picking up your head to see beyond your nose!

After you are given these instructions and told to ring the call light if you have to use the bedpan (and you will have to use it frequently due to the fluids they push through your veins to help your kidneys), you are then granted a food tray.

Having been NPO (nothing per mouth) for hours, you find yourself very hungry. If the kitchen gets it right, the food tray sent up should consist of finger-friendly foods—food that easily can be eaten from a prone position with your fingers.

The second heart cath to repair a blockage opened up a new world for me. I never thought I would become an expert at handling the aftermath. I was brought back to my room and slid back onto my bed. Given the instructions once more, I buckled down for an eight-hour session of flatness. The nurse handed me my call button and told me the kitchen was sending up a food tray. I was relieved the worse was over and looking forward to some substance for my grumbling stomach.

The food tray arrived pretty fast and the food service worker set it on my bed table, aligning it so I could reach the contents. She left and I uncovered the plate. Under that brown, airtight, insulated top was a bowl—a bowl of steaming hot soup! How did they expect me to eat soup? There was a spoon on the tray, the nurses were in the middle of shift change, and I was hungry. So spoon in hand I dipped into the soup and guided it to my mouth, trying to keep a flat angle. I carefully lowered the spoon over my mouth, but the soup dribbled down my neck, leaving behind bits of carrots and celery, not to mention the uncomfortable sensation of a wet hospital gown and pillowcase. After a few attempts, a nurse came in and was surprised at my dilemma.

"Why did they give you soup?" she exclaimed. "I'll call down to get you another tray with finger food."

"Thank you," was my reply. I hoped it wouldn't take too long.

Another tray of food was delivered. By now my doctor had come in to check on me. She was my endocrinologist and was concerned about my blood sugar levels and hospital diet. Now remember, I was in a room on the advanced cardiac care unit.

After chatting a bit, she said, "Here, why don't I help you with your food? Hopefully this time it won't be soup!" She uncovered the plate of food and we both stared in shock. Under that insulated, plastic, brown, cover was a gigantic mound of FRENCH FRIES! Soggy, greasy French fries! We both stared in shock. How could they serve French fries on a cardiac unit to a diabetic and in such a large quantity?

Of course she had the nurse come in and retrieve the tray. "When we order finger food for a heart patient, we don't mean French fries," was her response. "Please order another tray with appropriate food."

Once again the kitchen was contacted to send up the right food. One other thing I always do in the hospital is order a vegetarian diet. Not because I am a full-time vegetarian, but have you noticed what kind of meat they serve in a hospital? It's known as mystery meat, and I prefer not even to have to smell it arriving in my room.

Another tray came up, and they tried to accommodate my being vegetarian. But the only thing on the tray was a bunch of cut up carrots and celery—and nothing else. I was hoping for maybe some cheese or, hey, a sandwich might be a novel idea. When the nurse saw the meager vegetables, she asked me what I wanted to do.

"Tell them I am a vegetarian but I don't want only vegetables. Ask them to send me a vegetarian tray with more than vegetables."

Up came the final tray. The nurse brought it in with four of her colleagues following her in a procession. Everyone wanted to see what was going to be under the cover this time.

Someone hummed a drum roll.

The food was placed on my bed table. I stared intensely at the tray. My right arm reached over to grab the cover. All eyes were on the plate and, in one swoop, I lifted the cover and there was, to everyone's shock, a large heaping plate of MIXED vegetables, cooked and piled high.

I was so done. I wanted no more attempts from the kitchen! I called my dear friend Terry and begged her to bring me some real food. She arrived thirty minutes later with tacos. I ate them without guilt. After all, the hospital food was going to either kill me or starve me!

Lesson learned: Bring your own food if you are admitted to a hospital! But be careful about how you sneak in forbidden food …

Terry, being a faithful friend who has gone beyond incomprehensible limits to help me in any way, was famous for bringing items like Dairy Queen's Peanut Buster Parfait or, once in a while, a good old-fashioned cheeseburger and French fries. I had my share of healthy food—so occasionally a little junk food was good for my morale!

Normally if she brought me a Peanut Buster Parfait, she could sneak it in pretty easily. All I had to do was bury the empty container deep enough in the garbage pail and brush my teeth to get rid of the smell of ice cream on my breath.

On one occasion, when Terry brought me a cheeseburger and fries, she tried to be careful but the hospital chaplain for the cardiac floor saw her deliver the goods to my room. Immediately, he ran to my dietician to blab about my altercation. From then on, Terry would disguise my booty in a gift bag sealed in a Ziploc!

What about embarrassing moments throughout the many inpatient visits? You will laugh—or maybe cry. Like the flying bedpan story. (If you are squeamish, skip the next few paragraphs.)

I was lying flat after one of my many heart caths and it came time to use the bedpan. Hospitals have some odd idea that their new bedpans are more efficient. Maybe for storage, but the new plastic ones are way too small. So I always ask for the old-fashioned metal bedpan.

This particular time, I had a nurse's aide who wasn't familiar with my routine. The other aide would sprinkle some powder on the metal bedpan to avoid it sticking to me. This aide could not find any powder and offered some hand cream.

"I'm not sure that is a good idea," I cautioned.

"Oh, it will work fine," she replied confidently. I wasn't worried about it *not* working, but actually working *too* well.

She placed the bedpan, coated with hand cream, under my body. Within a second of my lying back on it, the metal pan slid out from under me and went flying through the air, past her and my husband, and hit the wall. After it crashed to the floor, we all looked for a moment and then burst out laughing. A bit of advice: no hand cream on a bedpan!

Then there are roommates and occupants adjacent to the hospital rooms I occupied. Since my heart transplant, I am confined to a private, germ-free isolation room. But before that I had some roommates with whom I played antics. After a while, that earned me a private room and usually the one right across from the nurse's station where they could keep an eye on me.

During one of my earlier visits I had a roommate close to my age who wasn't morbidly ill but was recovering from a heart procedure. Hating the humiliating hospital gowns they give you to wear, she wanted to get a set of scrubs to wear instead. (Scrubs consist of a top and pants and are not issued to patients. They are highly sought after when you are stuck in a hospital for a while.)

"Don't worry, Theresa, I will get you some scrubs," I said.

"How?" she asked me.

"Watch." I pressed the call button and my nurse came by to see what I needed.

"Can I help you, Cindy?" he asked. "He" was Mark, a tall, good-looking RN with a great personality.

"Yeah, can you send in Laura?" Laura was another nurse who had worked with me on a previous visit. Mark looked puzzled but sent her in. I whispered something in her ear and she looked at me like I was crazy.

"Do you know how hard it is to get those? I can't even get a set if I wanted them for myself, let alone a patient!" She turned around and stormed out, yelling back that she would see what she could do.

Theresa asked me how I got to her to try. "Oh, I have some dirt on her that wouldn't sit well with the head nurse," I told her. "She will get us the scrubs or I will have to turn her in." Theresa looked bewildered. I smirked at the joy of such mischief.

Not an hour later, Laura was back with two neatly wrapped, freshly cleaned sets of scrubs. She threw them down on my bed. "Here, am I free now?" she snapped at me with a hint of a smile on her lips.

"OK, you're off the hook. But don't let anyone in here while we change!"

I went over to Theresa's bed and started to help her change into her scrubs. It was crazy to get the top and pants on with all the tubing and IVs to which she was hooked up. She was getting out of breath and I was worried she might have another heart attack.

"Maybe I should give this up," I said. "You're having a hard time breathing!"

"Oh, no," she replied. "I am so excited to have these instead of that terrible gown. I am not giving them up now!"

I got her all dressed and back in her bed. As I started getting out of my gown and into my set of scrubs, Mark walked back in. There I was with the pants halfway up and the shirt entangled in my IV tubing.

"What in the world are you doing? And where did you get those scrubs? And why is your roommate's heart rate so fast?" Trying to answer without laughing so hard, I told him I made a deal with someone to get us scrubs. Of course I wouldn't tell him who. Nor would Theresa or I give up our scrubs. He was so mad!

We both stayed in those scrubs for three days. We finally stank so bad we had to give them up. But for a time, we had a small piece of victory and independence! Tip: You may have to wear a hospital gown because of all the tubing they poke into you, but at least bring your own underwear and pajama pants.

I spent so many long hours in my hospital room that I became creative with projects to keep myself busy. At one point, I satisfied the urge to better the stay for other patients by creating a David Letterman-type list to distribute to those whose hospital stays extended beyond a tolerant limit.

The Top Ten Reasons You Know You've Been in the Hospital Too Long

10
You press the call button and instead of "Can I help you?" the nurse asks on a first name basis, "Can I help you, *Cindy*?"

9
You hope to graduate from a bedpan to a bedside commode so you can have your very own personal roll of toilet paper.

8
The lab technician flicks on the lights at four A.M. and you're sitting up in bed with your arm outstretched and fist clenched tightly.

7

The bell signaling food service is on the floor causes you
a mad rush to clear your bedside tray and return your pillows
to an upright position.

6

The sound of the shower running in the room next to you triggers
severe jealousy as you sponge bath yourself in hopes of one day
gaining the privilege of a real shower.

5

When the volunteer comes around with a cart full of activities and
reading materials, you choose a "bored" game to play with your
invisible friend.

4

During the half hour of bingo on the hospital's TV channel, you
refuse all treatments or nursing requests as you frantically
search for G57.

3

You keep a chart to calculate how many turkey sandwiches the
hospital serves per day.

2

You recognize the nurse's footsteps—and time it just right so you can
salt your mashed potatoes and hide the saltshaker before she comes
back.

And the number one reason you know you've been in the hospital
too long:

1

You open the small closet in your room and an avalanche of packaged
saltine crackers, graham crackers, and packets of salt and sugar you
collected come tumbling down on your head!

There actually have been funny sides to all the painful times. And my lasting legacy is a fitting title assigned to me by one of the transport personnel at the hospital. I had an alternate ego that I appropriately displayed with a gold tiara, red cloak, and jeweled scepter. Whenever I was allowed to walk the hallways on the cardiac unit, I placed my tiara on my head, draped my red silk cape over my drab hospital gown, and toted my scepter, being sure to knight whomever I saw in the hallways. It worked great when I was in the hospital for Halloween on several occasions.

One time when I was walking about, I spotted an unknown doctor at the nurse's station. Walking up to him with royal flare, I used my scepter to knight him and declared him "Sir Doctor." He turned pale, slowly backed up, and made his way to the elevators. I guess he didn't have a sense of humor.

Well, you gotta laugh!

CHAPTER 7

I Am Who I Am

"YOU WILL BE trading one set of problems for another, but you will be alive." That's the proclamation I received from my transplant coordinator and surgeon before my heart transplant.

Their statement felt rehearsed and matter-of-fact. Like a flat line on an EKG monitor, it was final and its delivery took away the hope of ever getting better. I wanted to live, but the promise of new, unknown problems left a hollow gap in my expectations. Still, I so desperately was fighting for my life that I didn't care what trade-off I had to make.

After my transplant, I was waiting in line to board a plane when a girl asked me a poignant question.

A pink surgical mask covered most of my face. When I exhaled from under its protection, warm breath fogged up my glasses. Hung from my neck with thick, beige string was a bold and defiant sign. The words *Heart Transplant—Germs make me sick* were printed in big red letters overlapping a picture of a heart and stethoscope. I felt empowered to handle the onslaught of stares as long as I hid behind its barrier. (I am finally over the phobia and now travel without a label.)

"Did you ever feel like you would have rather died?" she asked. "I mean, if I was in your situation, I think I would rather have died than to live with all the hassles you endure. I am not married and don't have any children, so I guess it makes a difference."

Her question was honest and viable.

I stood there for a moment, watching her eyes look deep into mine, her silhouette standing out among the throngs of people crowded at the gate. Thoughts raced in my head like Data on Star Trek attempting to calculate the exact answer. I wanted to give her a perfect reply. But I didn't have one for myself. I couldn't comprehend a different choice.

Would I rather have died than go through a heart transplant?

I answered her but wasn't sure myself.

"Well, I have a husband and a teenage son who need me. I wanted to be here for them." She looked at me quizzically and pondered my answer.

"I guess that makes sense," she replied. We boarded the plane.

I always think about her question. Sometimes I am so worn out from all the health problems, appointments, insurance claims and hassles, medications and their side effects, not being able to physically do things I like, daily struggles, and the ominous shadow of my shortened lifespan that I waver a bit on my decision to choose to live.

But the thought usually is snuffed out when I think of how selfish it would be to want to avoid all the struggles and leave behind no good testimony of what God can do when we trust Him for each day's battle. Although I am different physically, I am still who I am.

When I travel, I have to wear a mask marking me as different and, to some people, as a possible threat. In fact, quite often people inevitably will decide I am some contagious creature and change their seats, avoid me, cover their own faces, or ask something insulting.

One day I stood in line at the deli counter, my stomach growling from hunger. It was amazing to shop on my own, without a wheelchair or someone to help. After getting a few groceries, I planned to go home and make dinner—another formidable accomplishment.

The crisp, perfectly browned chicken strips stared out from the glass case. I inhaled the aroma and tapped my foot on the tile floor, eager to place my order.

The woman in line ahead of me turned around, her heavy winter coat draped across her arm. Her eyes fixed on my pink mask. I was secretly smiling underneath.

"Are you sick?" she demanded.

"No, I had a heart transplant and have to wear this mask so I don't get sick myself."

She remained focused on my mask.

"But I don't want to get sick," she continued. "I just can't get sick."

"I am not sick."

Throwing her coat back over her shoulders, she turned and hastily left the store with her hand covering her mouth.

I went up to the counter to place my order and the deli clerk smiled.

"I guess it can come in handy, having a heart transplant," I said, smirking at the absurdity.

I was different. When I became a Christian, I was different. I worried about how to change who I was and what I was. I internalized much about myself and scurried around using way too many sharp edges to do my own pruning in hopes of being the best Christian I could be.

God got hold of me on certain occasions. He has a way of taking sometimes the quietest moment, or the simplest environment, and using the time to make a tremendous statement.

One warm summer night on Lake Coeur d'Alene in Idaho, He did just that.

The crescent moon hung low in the dark evening sky amid stars positioned in their appointed places. A caressing breeze rippled over the deck as our cruise ship meandered along the velvet, peaceful lake. I looked around through dimly lit groups of people—some were sitting and singing as praise and worship choruses undulated from the musicians at the bow of the ship. Others stood, faces toward the horizon and hands raised in peaceful worship. The evening was surreal.

The melodic phrases of "Amazing Grace" were being sung when suddenly lights appeared in the sky—the Northern Lights. Colors danced and shifted against the black sky as nature's light show hung down like majestic draperies. The Northern Lights can only be seen at certain times of the year and conditions must be right for them to appear. I always had wanted to witness their unearthly phenomenon. For most of us, the appearance of such a natural wonder was the perfect ending to a perfect evening.

But as I stood in the midst of this entire splendor, tears streamed down my cheeks. I was struggling to hold back a torrent of weeping emotions. The ship, a dinner cruise reserved for our church group, held four hundred people. Both the top and bottom decks were filled. With people all around me, there was nowhere to escape. I tried my hardest to hide the pain that was trying to gush forth from inside my tormented soul. What was a beautiful evening for most became the finalization of a work the Lord had started in me years before. I had arrived that night at the furthest point of control—the emptiest part of my own self-realization.

Leaving the ship, I made it to our car without anyone noticing how much I had cried. I looked over at my husband and asked, "How do you know when you've had an emotional breakdown?"

He looked at me, puzzled by the abrupt question. "Why do you ask?"

"I think I had one tonight." My reply was straight-out. The rest of the drive home was in silence. But once we got our son to bed and sat down with a cup of tea, the tears began and I sobbed the innermost nuggets of pain from my broken heart. All the issues from my past—that is, my Christian past, of which I took control and rid myself—were being paraded in front of me one by one. The Lord grabbed each circumstance and held it up to my face, letting me know there was trash onto which I was holding tightly. For the first time, I clearly could see my problem with control. I sought to control my life, my spiritual state, my circumstances, my purpose, and even my destiny. For someone who thought she had let go of all control, I now realized I was safely hiding the last fragments of my own domination.

What I did with many issues throughout the years was to conquer them on my own and neatly tuck them away. The problem with such annihilation is that a complete ridding of bitterness, scars, anger, sin, unforgiveness, and other roots of hurt cannot happen unless the Lord gets complete control. I read all the scriptures about forgiveness. I paid attention to the deep sermons on letting go, and I profusely studied how to grow close to the Lord to let Him control my life. When I confidently awarded myself with an A+ for passing the school of letting go, He stripped me down to bare my soul and expose my folly.

Where did the intense desire to control my life come from? I can see the dynamite in memories as far back as my childhood.

"Let go of her, Laura, or I'll deck you one." My voice was strengthened with anger and vengeance as I lunged toward the assailant. Laura's fists were swinging as she aimed at Sara, a much smaller and younger girl. Being a tomboy and bully, Laura easily could inflict the harm she intended on her victim.

"Oh, no, you don't," I asserted as I grabbed Laura's neck and yanked her off Sara.

Turning Laura around, I pinned her against the wall of our cabin and began to hurl punches at her—hitting and missing in my moment of fury. Her feet dangled off the wooden floor as she struggled to get free of my grip. Considering I was much smaller than her, it was amazing I could keep her prisoner to my attack.

"Cynthia! What on earth are you doing to that poor girl?" I can still hear the camp counselor's exasperated yell. She pulled me away as Laura's body sunk to the floor. Huddled in a bundle of tears, Laura pointed at me, yelling out in anger that I had started the whole fight.

We were both marched to the main office, where a senior counselor ironed out the truth and instructed us to hug and make up. Hours later, Laura was planning another assault while the rest of us sang around a roasting campfire. I watched my back in anticipation of a secret attack.

I was only ten years old when I first realized the power of my anger and wrath and the unending desire to control what surrounded me. Being raised with twelve siblings in New York, combined with the volatility of an Italian heritage, destined me to be a neatly packaged stick of dynamite. Wholehearted causes, arguments, the need for survival, and everyday struggles of life in a large family bred the instinct to control and shape my surroundings.

My husband, barely seventeen when I latched onto him, became the object of my desire to gain control and comfort. I looked to him to fulfill my shortcomings—the areas where I had no reins to steer and direct.

We married six years after John first asked me to go steady. Our relationship appeared to be the perfect courtship. Even the circumstances for his proposal were cleverly manipulated by my need to move out from the clutches of my home life. I became the decision maker and controller. I did not allow my husband to take his place as spiritual leader and head of our household. Overwhelmed by my dominating design, he became reclusive, leaving me to deal with all the matters of our marriage. It made for an unbalanced and insecure relationship.

When our son came along and financial and medical problems mounted, I demanded that John step in and fix everything. But I had created a lopsided relationship that needed drastic measures to be righted. With much heartbreak, we sought the help of a Christian counselor. After several sessions, this gentle, gracious counselor looked at me with intent and said, "You have to let go of your desire to control everything. Let your husband be who he needs to be in this marriage." I instantly was deflated. Had I really taken control? Hadn't I given up the "old me" a long time ago when I asked Jesus to be my Lord? No, there was much more to the cleansing than I ever could foresee. This was merely a small advance to be rid of a deep-rooted cause.

I have learned that many times when we struggle with an area of our lives we cannot overcome, giving it to the Lord may entail a multifaceted process. Our Lord is a creative God who knows each of us intimately. If we allow Him to be the One who conquers our hurdles, it will be complete—He will not leave a trace to take root and become an issue for us again. God's cleansing is complete and perfect.

In my mind, I still can see the Northern Lights from that evening. They spread their color and radiated through the black sky dotted with stars. After twenty minutes or so, they blended softly into the dark horizon.

I can be who I am. My identity is not lost in Christ but celebrated through Him. There is much power in a person who is not in control. Opposite as it may be to the world's thinking, there is One who can do a much better job at leading our lives through the foreign world we live in. When I was a young girl, I dreamed of becoming the first woman president. And I am—president of my place in God's perfect plan for my life. I sit at the top with His arm over my shoulder, pointing out the glorious way He has put together my days.

I often think of how many times I avoided meeting new people after I got sick. I didn't want anyone to know the new me. I wanted them to know who I was and what I could do before heart disease crippled me. I was afraid I had lost the person I was to someone who was disabled and trodden down. I no longer had the qualities I once had possessed. It took me a long time to emerge from my own ashes and peek out at a different life ahead of me. I am still struggling to resist the desire to hide from the world.

In the February 2008 edition of the AHA's *Heart Insight Magazine*, Kathleen Prentice writes about how her life changed after surviving an unexpected heart attack while caring for her children and aging parents. She titles one section in her article "When a Caregiver Needs Care" as "The New Normal" and writes:

> My life had changed from being a biker and swimmer to feeling grateful to be able to walk from the sofa to the shower by myself, grateful to be home, grateful to be alive, grateful to share a laugh with my daughter. ... I felt like I had relinquished control over my job description, my identity. ... I had to accept letting Bob, Caitlin, and younger daughter, Lily, take over the household and my care—and to accept how they did it. ... What I wanted most of all, was to return to normal. What we've ended up with is a blend of pre-and-post heart attack routines. A new normal.[55]

A *new normal* is not always what we want normal to be. So many things can change and our lives can become a state of bedlam. After one of my many ER visits, my son, then thirteen years old, asked, "This is never going to end, is it?" His normal was long gone.

One day when I picked him up from school, I saw he had a failing test grade. I asked him, "What do you think about all day, Jonathan?"

His answer broke my already frail heart. "Mom, I never know if you are going to be dead or alive when I get home from school." His view of me took on a very different form.

"Normal" was forever changed one day for Joni Eareckson-Tada, as she shares in her book *Joni*. You might remember her story. In 1967, Joni, a teenager enjoying summer break, suffered a diving accident that left her paralyzed from the neck down. Her ministry, Joni and Friends, has since touched people both with and without disabilities all over the world.

In the book she explains how she came to terms with struggling over her self-image:

> I'd still look at healthy, active people—attractive people—enjoying themselves around me. Everyone I compared myself to came out best. I'd even lose out when I compared myself to a mannequin!

> My friend Steve answered my quandary, "But that's the same for everyone if we let society determine our value. We always lose if we evaluate ourselves according to someone else's ideas or standards. And there are as many standards as there are people. We have to forget about what people say or think and recognize that God's values are the only important ones."

> It was true. God knew that I had hands and feet and arms and legs that did not work. He knew what I looked like. And none of these things really mattered. What counted was that I was His workmanship created in His image. And He wasn't finished with me (Eph. 2:10).[56]

"He wasn't finished with me." Joni's words make me think of how often I wanted to go back to being the "old" me. But that is what the past is—old, and I needed, and still need, to realize I am "new." I am a new person with new direction.

One day I met someone who has forever changed my life and caused me to keep my eyes off the past.

I sat up on the stiff hospital bed, pillows propped behind me, and watched out the door. Several people had gathered to offer encouragement. Among the group, I noticed a remarkable young man in a black electric wheelchair. He motored through the door, his big sunny smile lighting up the room.

Jeff said he had heard about John and me and wanted to come and pray with us. More important to me was John would have someone with whom to talk and to wait. Jeff watched and seemed to ponder as John spoke to him. It was clear he was interested in John—interested in how he was doing. I was content to see someone there for John and not just me.

Soon after that first meeting, Jeff "typed" me an e-mail. I emphasize "typed" because Jeff's wheelchair confinement is due to the loss of both his arms and the use of his legs in an electrocution accident several years ago when he was only thirty. He types with the ends of each claw attached where his hands should be. It's a long process for him to get through typing one page.

At the time he had his accident, Jeff, a thirty year old owner of a successful billboard maintenance company, had a family of five children, the youngest being only thirteen days old. It was three days before Christmas and Jeff was singing Christmas carols, thinking of bringing his children to visit Santa. He was up on a billboard, forty feet high, when his equipment came into contact with an electrical line that was out of place. Over 14,400 bolts of electricity burned through his body, and he was killed instantly.

When his body fell to the ground, the impact started his heart back up. Barely alive, he died again while being flown by plane to a trauma center three hundred miles away. Miraculously, he lived through the first few critical days, even though he was not expected to make it. The ensuing year was spent in painful rehabilitation.

As it now stands, he has limited use of his battered legs, he wears two prosthetic arms with claws that are controlled by straps attached to his back, and he endures severe pain every moment of each day and long night.

Below is his letter to me, in his own words, from November 2003:

Dear Cindy,

Don't you just hate being a human ... I know that I do sometimes! I went through that a little bit ... with we're going to cut this off ... No, we're going to try and save it ... many times over. Like you, I'm a pretty positive person ... and ultimately trust God and His will ... Unfortunately I had my down times, troubled times, and angry times ... And that hellish roller coaster ride just consumed me, and prolonged the bad times, so that they were outnumbering and outlasting the positive times. This is what I ultimately decided ... and it may not be for you ... it just worked for me. I took all of the trust and hope that I had placed in docs, circumstances, luck, and my own strength ... and cleared it out.

I also had several weeks with a life-threatening infection near my spine ... They tried everything, they were opening me up at least once a week and cutting away the infected tissue ... I was on the most powerful antibiotic known to man ... nothing was working ... it looked like the infection was going to be fatal. I know that it probably sounds morbid ... it does to me ... as I type ... but I went ahead and said Lord, it doesn't look like I'll make it ... please give me peace about dying ... I would just ask that You use me until then. It worked!

I read a lot of Paul's writings ... We can both relate to him ... I played a couple of songs frequently ... my favorite was "My Hope Is in You" ... by Third Day ... Eventually they put antibiotic beads near my spine, and I got through it. I made my peace with losing ALL of my limbs, at the torso ... When they stopped at an elbow, and just below my shoulder ... I was thrilled! Even though they had hopes (which were contagious) of preserving more. At least for me ... I was still able to be positive ... because I was vigilantly watching for that one opportunity where God could use me.

I didn't get pre-occupied with death, or dwell on it ... I just made the most of the time I had with my family ... I didn't tell them about my mindset ... they wouldn't have understood ... and would have thought that I was throwing in the towel, and been hurt and upset. They would have spent all of our time together trying to talk me out of my new perspective.

The bottom line is that God honored it ... He did use me, and He was glorified. So now ... any development short of death ... doesn't surprise me ... No, I'm not the picture of joy that I think Paul was ... but it enables me to deal with it nonetheless.

After my accident, when I woke up after eight days ... I realized that I had a big house payment, a minivan payment, and two truck payments from my business ... no savings, no disability, and putrid medical insurance ... five young kids to feed ... It was way beyond me ... it was totally hopeless for me ... so I had no option other than giving it ALL completely over to God ... He handled everything in His timing ... paid off the vehicles, and then the house ... with less than five hundred dollars left over ... it was beautiful.

I really was fortunate ... because I could've/would've worked out a plan if it was humanly possible ... after all, I worked harder than anyone I knew. I was a successful businessman, I even built my own home ... If anyone could do it ... I could. My situation was so ridiculously impossible ... I didn't have a choice ... but I did have a prayer ... a prayer of desperation and faith ... God rose to the challenge, and met our needs in such a miraculous way ... that it affected hundreds of people ... and still does when I tell my story to a group ... it literally changed people's lives.

I can honestly say, Cindy ... that if I was in a similar situation as you guys (I don't know everything) but a scenario in which there was a glimmer of hope ... I wouldn't have been able to give it to God 100 percent ... I would have missed the miracle and blessing ... and so would have hundreds ... maybe thousands of others. So I just want to encourage you to relax ... spend some time reminding yourself of God's promises ... I'm in this with you guys for the looong haul ... eternity. I am blessed and encouraged immeasurably by spending time with you.

I pray for you guys every time God puts you on my heart ... I imagine that those are the down times for you ... anyway ... I'm wearing out the sharp end of my hook with all of this typing.

Love you guys,
Jeff [57]

Jeff had so much life to live and so much to look forward to, and now he looks forward to getting through each day. His youthful body, now prisoner to the physical trauma, drains his days with pain and helplessness. People stare at the plastic replacements for his hard-working, muscular arms and the claws that act as hands. But Jeff keeps his sense of humor, offering opening lines like, "Hi, I'm Jeff. Shake my claw!"

Does Jeff's appearance change who he is? People look at him with preexisting ideas of his worth. But Jeff is stronger and better than he ever was. His worth to God is more valuable with a broken body as long as his heart is sustained only by God's power.

A similar story of visible transformation occurred for Greg Gadson. Gadson, a brawny, determined athlete for the Army football team, was returning from memorial services for two soldiers from his battalion when a roadside bomb hit the truck in which he was traveling. A lieutenant colonel in the Army's Warrior Transition Brigade, Gadson lost both his legs in the accident, and never would play football again. Though he faced life from the sidelines, physically it did not stop him from being a team player and being given credit for leading the New York Giants to a Super Bowl victory in 2007.

A former schoolmate at West Point, now a coach for the New York Giants, went to see Gadson in the hospital:

> The coach watched as Gadson interacted with the other patients and the doctors and nurses, encouraging them all. "To see the impact he had on these people—the look in his eyes and how they responded—was overwhelming and inspirational."

> When the Giants were scheduled to play the Redskins in Washington three months later, Sullivan [the coach] sent his friend tickets—along with a request: Would Gadson speak to the team before they took the field? Having lost the first two games of the season, the Giants had already given up eighty points and, worse, seemed to be playing with no heart. The coach felt that Gadson was the perfect person to tell the players something they needed to hear about commitment, about perseverance, about teamwork.

> The Giants were a losing team until Gadson gave them the heart to win.[58]

It is people like Gadson who can tell their story of tragedy and instill the desire in others to grow into who God made them to be.

In the fall of 1974, Tim Hansel went from a healthy, strong, vibrant lifestyle to one of constant pain after a climbing accident while scaling the Sierras. Tim relates to the tragedy of losing who he was and living with pain and constraints on a daily basis. He took strong advice from his doctor and found himself finally free to be who God made him to be:

> "Son, listen to me carefully. The damage has been done. My recommendation is that you live your life as fully and richly as possible. Bite the bullet and live to be a hundred. As far as I can tell, you can do whatever the pain will allow you to do."

> I left with a new lease on life, a resurgent hope for the future, and a new commitment to live life again with a sense of abandonment.

> As strange as it may seem, up to that point I hadn't known I had a choice. I had allowed myself to step into the victim mentality without wanting it or knowing it. But through a gentle doctor, our Lord again "turned my mourning into dancing, and my sackcloth into joy" (Ps. 30:11).[59]

A friend once asked me how I was able to stay as upbeat as I was and keep my personality intact after all I had suffered and continue to suffer. My reply was a simple numerical value: 0. I had to get myself out of the way, make myself a 0, and let God be 100 percent of my strength. No, I did not lose who I was or become incapable of fighting for myself. But the only fighting I had to do was to fight off self.

"God is in the midst of her, she will not be moved" (Ps. 46:5 NASB). As long as God makes up 100 percent of me, I shall not be moved by whatever comes at me.

There's a pain scale used in all hospitals and clinics called the "Faces of Pain." The numbers to rate your pain go from zero to ten, with ten being the worst. I like to think of the scale as my self-meter. When my self is at a zero, I am joyful and happy because God is in complete control.

When my self is at ten, the joy is gone as I have taken the control away from God and tried to get through the pain without Him.

I now have a new physical heart, but its life expectancy is unsure compared to most people's hearts. This new heart beats with distrustful promise of supporting my body's demand for blood and oxygen—the life flow it needs to survive. Yet I must lean solely on God to provide my every breath. I constantly evaluate each moment and regard my life as one that belongs to God. Surrendered to His will for my life, I give God all He wants—the "I am" of my soul, the all of my spiritual heart. I am still who I am even though people may judge me physically or by my abilities. God molded me into who I am meant to be. He must be at the top of my scale.

As I waited for a donor heart to become available, I often wondered about who might end up being the donor. Knowing someone had to die for me to live placed an awkward stigma on my desiring a life-saving transplant. And part of the strangeness was the feeling of having someone else's heart beating inside me. It comes to me as a much-venerated occurrence.

Charles Siebert, a medical writer who frequently contributes to *The New York Times Magazine,* writes the following after attending a party held for more than a hundred heart transplant recipients:

> All the people I met at the party spoke in the same reverent tones about the angel in their chests, about this gift, this responsibility they now bear, and the little prayer they say to the other person inside of them.[60]

I knew my heart donor only as a twenty-eight-year-old young woman. Because of privacy and respect, the donor and recipient families are protected from being contacted by each other's families and friends.

But as the recipient, I was allowed to write a letter signed with my first name only that did not include any other details of my identity. An office representing the organ donation foundation where the donor lived would deliver the letter to the appropriate donor family member.

I wrote a letter three months after my transplant. It was difficult to know what to say. I kept it short, mailed it, and prayed and hoped for a chance to get to know more about my donor. As Siebert says in his article, there is a reverence for the person whose heart now beats in your chest. I felt a connection to whoever this woman was and I had a strong yearning to meet her family—whoever they were.

Late one Friday at work, I decided to call the Donate Life Today! office in Seattle. (Their office worked with my donor's family.) It was 4:45 P.M. so I wasn't sure anyone would answer.

Valerie answered the phone. "Hello, Cindy, it's good to hear from you."

My voice was shaky. "I was wondering if it would be too intrusive to write one more letter to my donor family. I don't want to upset them."

Valerie answered with excitement in her voice.

"Your donor's mom called a couple of days ago to see if she could find out how the person was who had gotten her daughter's heart," she told me.

"Do you think she may want to be in touch?" I asked with hesitation.

"It's a good sign. I will call her and let you know."

I hung up the phone and cried. "She has a mom," I kept walking around saying. "My donor has a mom." Knowing someone was out there and connected to the heart beating in my chest gave me a whole new feeling of urgency to find out who they were. I knew I had an extended family somewhere.

The next Monday, the coordinator called me. Charlotte, my donor's mom, wanted to get in touch! And her daughter's name, whose heart was beating in my chest, was Danielle. She told me she would be sending the permission papers to both of us to fill out and sign, and then we were free to contact each other. I was thrilled and excited about the chance to know more about Danielle's family.

In time, I began to talk with Charlotte on the phone. We cried mostly, laughed at similarities between her daughter and me, and finally planned to meet on Easter weekend. I learned that Danielle had three brothers and a step-dad. I also got to know Danielle and what led up to the tragic accident that took away her life but gave me mine back.

When Danielle was five years old, her dad was killed in a motorcycle accident, leaving Charlotte to raise three children on her own. They often had to visit the local food bank to get help with the family's needs. Danielle was so touched by the acts of kindness, she insisted to her mom that when she grew up she would "help others like they were helping them." As she grew, she did just that—gave whatever she had if someone she saw needed it. She gave away her coat to a friend and came home in the cold rain without it, her shoes were donated to a friend in need as she walked home barefoot, her lunch was often offered to another classmate who had nothing, and she always asked for extra snacks to hand out to those less fortunate.

As she got older, Danielle explained to her mom that she felt like she was put on the earth to give to those who were in need of help. When she got her driver's license, she decided to become an organ donor. "Mom, if something were to happen to me," she said, "why would I want my organs to be buried when someone's life could be saved or helped by me being a donor?"

No one likes to talk about a subject as sensitive as dying, but it was important to Danielle that her family knew her wishes. Then the tragic day came when, as Charlotte put it, "I lost something very dear to me—my little princess."

Danielle was an epileptic and had a seizure one day that caused her to slip and fall in the shower. She suffered a concussion and also hit her neck, cutting off blood flow to her brain from her carotid arteries in her neck. After three days in the hospital, all hope was lost that she ever would come back. When Charlotte was notified that the hospital called a code blue on Danielle, the code for eminent death, she was distraught. "Why God?" she asked. "Why are You doing this? Take me instead of her."

Danielle's brothers and the rest of her family all struggled with their loss. But Charlotte knew God had a purpose on earth for her daughter—her "princess." She also knew that if Danielle's organs had not been donated, there would have been no purpose to her death.

The holidays were always difficult for Charlotte, but after we talked for a few months, she agreed to meet my family and me on Easter weekend—almost three years after losing Danielle. It was an emotional and powerful meeting for both of us, Charlotte finding closure and me getting to know about the person whose heart was keeping me alive.

Charlotte said something only someone so close to the Lord could comprehend: "After getting to know you," she explained through tears of relief, "I now know that my daughter's purpose on earth was to be here so when you needed a new heart, she could give you hers."

How could a mom say something like that after losing her daughter? Danielle was a Christian, and she demonstrated it by her giving and loving lifestyle. And Danielle is still who she is, and I am who I am, but part of me has a piece of Danielle that God holds in high esteem—her heart. I cannot be who I am without Danielle's heart keeping me alive.

"But by the grace of God I am what I am" (1 Cor. 15:10). This verse is clipped onto the bulletin board in my kitchen, reminding me quite often of who I am in God's eyes. No matter what I do wrong, whatever pain I suffer, whatever failures I despair over, I am exactly who God made me to be. And it was His plan that Danielle's life would become part of mine.

I now have an extended family to which I am very connected. Besides the physical connection, there is an emotional connection and a spiritual connection. All of us have gone through difficult situations to be where God wanted us to be, but embracing the plan and purpose for our lives allows us to continue on His path and to remain faithful in His care.

You are exactly who God intended you to be also. Time and experience may mold you and smooth out the rough edges, but He made no mistake when He created you.

CHAPTER 8

Time Keeps on Ticking

Fly like an eagle, Let my spirit carry me
I want to fly like an eagle, Till I'm free
Oh, Lord, through the revolution

Time keeps on slippin', slippin', slippin'
Into the future
Time keeps on slippin', slippin', slippin'
Into the future ...[61]

I GREW UP in New York and learned to live in the craziness of its daily grind. I didn't have a chance to think about time. You knew a fifteen-mile trip in rush hour traffic would take forty-five minutes. A visit to register your car at the Department of Motor Vehicles included a three- to five-hour wait.

The express line at the grocery store was the longest line, so even though the amount of groceries per order was less, the time waiting was not. Emergencies were not shielded from the lack of time. If you had to visit the ER, you could count on a five-hour wait—unless your emergency was life threatening.

"The City That Never Sleeps," New York City's distinctive motto, is relative to its twenty-four-hour subway system and constant drones of traffic and people. Living there is a blur. Now that I live in a smaller city with rush hour traffic lasting five to ten minutes, I have to say, time is more of a reality.

Time is a word given much reverence. We sing about it, wonder about it, lose it, want it, and need more of it. Many are familiar with the lines from Ecclesiastes 3, "There is a time for everything." King Solomon wrote this after he expounds on the concept of time: "Whatever is has already been, and what will be has been before; and God will call the past to account" (Ecc. 3:15 NIV).

What is the importance of time and why do we mull over the past, worry about the present, and anticipate and plan the future? Why do we always need more of it? So we can fill it with things we must do, necessary restraints our lives impress on us.

We think of time lost in the past and mourn it. "If only I had …" The past is a part of our lives, and the Lord takes into account what we do with our lives here on earth, but "there is no time like the present." We can be responsible only for what happens today. We plan our futures the best we can, we work to make each day better than the one before, and we can only hope what we do brings the best result.

King Solomon contemplated how man works and plans and counts the minutes he wished he had: "So I saw that there is nothing better for a man than to enjoy his work, because that is his lot. For who can bring him to see what will happen after him?" (Eccl. 3:22 NIV). His is a sobering look at time and its passing.

After moving away from New York, and being gone almost ten years, my husband and I returned for a visit. We forgot how treacherous it is to drive the speed limit there even in the far right lane. I'm not sure how many times we were forced to go faster or be escorted out of the lane we were in. It's how New York and other large cities around the world operate.

A friend riding with us one day became impatient with my husband's driving. He was tormented that we took our time in the store, mulled about the shops we visited, and stopped to admire our surroundings. "You guys are no longer *engaged* in life!" was his outbreak. Honest and frustrated, his words are something to consider.

Engaged in life? Engaged is associated with being busy, occupied, or involved in conflict. People who are engaged with life are sometimes engrossed with their days.

Think about people who are terminally ill, divorced, financially ruined, raising rebellious children, dealing with broken relationships, or agonizing over unfulfilled promises and torn dreams—how much time do they need to find peace? How much time is enough to drive them to their goals or desires?

I have learned to pass over the quantity of time in my own life. I don't worry anymore about being engaged in life. Instead, I am determined to be absorbed with life, knowing how precious every chance is to work and live and be productive. "Behold, we count them happy which endure. Ye have heard of the patience of Job, and have seen the end of the Lord; that the Lord is very pitiful, and of tender mercy" (James 5:11 KJV).

I was working on a computer project at home one day for a ministry where I was employed, and something in the program would shut down each time I was ready to complete it. Just as I would be at the very end, the screen would blink—and it was gone! I was becoming frustrated when I realized I needed to take a breath and pray. I did. Then I rebooted the computer to give it a break. As I looked at the screen booting up and launched my program again, I anticipated another failure.

Suddenly, the Lord spoke loudly to me, "You may be doing the work, but I am doing the miracle!" It was loud and clear that I needed to rest and stop rushing the time.

Leaving my office, I walked outside to fill the bird feeders in my backyard. It was a cold winter day and the crisp air cleared my head. The birds were so hungry, they filled the trees around me with chatter and anticipation.

"Time," the Lord spoke to me, "is not a concern of Mine and should not be allowed to consume you. Use it wisely."

A few days later, my Bible reading for the day was supposed to be Psalm 7, but something led me to read Psalm 30. There was no particular reason—I just felt like the Lord wanted me to read it. As usual, it was perfect timing. Psalm 30 is all about God's promises. And they were promises I needed to hear.

O LORD my God, I cried unto thee, and thou hast healed me. O
LORD, thou hast brought up my soul from the grave: thou hast kept
me alive, that I should not go down to the pit. Hear, O LORD, and
have mercy upon me: LORD, be thou my helper. Thou hast turned
for me my mourning into dancing: thou hast put off my sackcloth,
and girded me with gladness.

—Ps. 30:2-3,10-11 KJV

I questioned when these things would happen: healing, keep me
alive, mercy, dancing, and gladness. Time has no meaning to God. If
I could grasp this fact and keep my thoughts from straying from the
truth, I would not have to worry anymore about timing. We have to
remember this and try to eliminate time in our prayers and requests.
Our future is the present to God.

Many of us have requests we would like answered in a timeframe we
can handle. For me, a new blockage could attack my coronary arteries.
My friend Jeff, electrocuted years ago—no arms, and in a wheelchair—
doesn't know how long he will live. How many countless people have
jobs without security? There are many with family members away at war
in foreign countries. The scenarios can go on endlessly if we consider
the way time makes itself an intrusion that demeans our faith. And we
can easily lose faith as we seem to lose time.

A tragic story appeared on February 9, 2008, as a tiny headline from
the Associated Press: "Bride dies during marriage's first dance":

Kim Sjostrom wanted a real-life version of the film "My Big Fat Greek
Wedding," which played in the background as friends fixed her hair
and makeup before her own marriage ceremony.

But less than an hour after she and Teddy Efkarpides were wed,
Sjostrom crumpled in her husband's arms during a Greek song that
means "Love Me."

At thirty-six, Sjostrom was dead from heart disease.

Sjostrom carried blue and white flowers during the ceremony—the
colors of the Greek flag—as she exchanged vows with Efkarpides, a

forty-three-year-old carpenter and Navy veteran. They had met three years to the day before the January 19 wedding.

During the couple's first dance, Sjostrom complained of being light-headed. Efkarpides thought his wife, a diabetic, needed sugar, but she collapsed.

Wedding guests, paramedics, and doctors at a nearby hospital were unable to revive her.

He [Efkarpides] consoles himself by reading a list of "101 Reasons Why I Love You" that Sjostrom gave him their first Christmas together. "Number 1. You make me smile."

No. 98 is especially difficult: "You're the one I want to grow old with."[62]

It's said that this couple never got to live out their lives as they planned. What might they have done differently if they had known their wedding day would be the last day they were together?

If all of us would consider the frailty of time, we probably would treat each other better. We would live our lives differently. The things that derail us no longer would have such disastrous effects on our emotions and choices. We can't know the future—even the next few minutes of time. But we can live our lives as if we do. As Francois de Fenelon says in *The Seeking Heart*:

Don't be so concerned about the future. The future belongs to God. He is in charge of all things and will take care of you completely. If you try to guess what is going to happen you will only worry yourself and anticipate trouble. Live each day as it comes.[63]

A few months after my heart transplant, time moved on a slow, surrealistic course. I was no longer counting how many days I waited for a donor heart to become available. I was simply—counting. *It's been three weeks*, I considered, *and I am still at the hospital several days at a time for X-rays, blood work, biopsies of my heart, appointments. ... I thought going home from the hospital meant the beginning of my new existence, my new lease on life. Instead, it is a new world with new conditions.*

Shortly after I was discharged from the hospital, the entourage of probing and testing began its assault. Living through a complicated heart transplant, my body felt like I was walking around after being mowed down by an eighteen-wheeler. Legs heavy, arms weak, insides screaming from pain—I wanted to go to bed and stay there.

But weekly hospital day trips, lasting three to six months, started a regular routine—biopsies, lab work, X-rays, and office visits. None of the appointments were in the same part of the hospital. Walking from one end to the other, outstretched hallways became unending, grueling corridors. Shiny floors to be traversed reflected up at me. Each step I took was an accomplishment.

I hated wheelchairs. But for these dreaded appointments, I wanted to be pushed rather than escorted.

After my transplant, my mom came to visit. She took me to my first checkup and grabbed a wheelchair for me, rolling me to the first stop.

"Mom, we can't let anyone from the transplant program see us."

"Why?" she asked.

"My coordinator told me not to let the doctors catch me using a wheelchair while I am here for testing. They want me to walk on my own." *Easy for a normal person to say,* was my angry thought.

My mom, a four-foot-eleven Italian powerhouse, pushed me from one appointment to another, adamant about making it easier on me.

The constant routine dragged me down and left me worn out with a lot of time to think. I know I dwelled on my situation more then I should have, more than was healthy for me. One thing that nagged at my disconcerted thoughts was, *Did I really need this heart transplant?* Four years of healthcare personnel doubting my condition had contributed to my own doubts. I wanted to know for sure.

At my next appointment, after all day testing, I was ready to see the heart transplant surgeon. I went through the nurse intake, weigh-in, and medication check, and waited for the doctor to come in. After his assessment, and the usual small talk, I asked him if I could speak to him privately.

"I have a question to ask you," I spoke softly as he looked into my eyes, probably searching for an indication of my state of mind.

We went into his back office. "Sit," he said.

"Oh no, that's OK. This will only take a moment." I was nervous about asking him a question I thought might make him feel awkward.

"Dr. Sandler, did I really need this heart transplant? I mean, so many times I was told things were in my mind. Would you and Dr. Icenogle have done this transplant if I hadn't needed it?"

His big brown Russian eyes looked at me with soothing mercy and love. He grabbed me and gave me his characteristic bear hug. Holding me tight, he spoke calmly, with his heavy accent. "Your heart was a capital 'G'—'G' for garbage. I don't know how you lasted as long as you did and you would not have lasted much longer."

That was what I needed to hear. My doubting came to an end. This man had had his hands in my chest. He had held my heart, the heart I was born with, and cut it out to replace it with a new heart. Although this new heart had physical impairments, it would come to beat strongly and keep me alive for much longer than any of us could know.

I am reminded of this message of hope each time I hear my heart beat. At night, when it is really quiet and I am lying in bed, I can hear and feel this new heart beating in my chest. It reminds me of Ezekiel's message of hope to God's people. Ezekiel chose always to obey God, and sometimes the things God asked him to do were dramatic and difficult. Still, Ezekiel continued to proclaim God's Word.

In Ezekiel 36:26, God promised to restore Israel not only physically but with a new spiritual heart:

> Moreover, I will give you a new heart and put a new spirit within you; and I will remove the heart of stone from your flesh and give you a heart of flesh. (NASB)

"Stony" is an interesting way to describe their prior hearts. When someone has had a lot of damage to his or her physical heart, the heart muscle becomes hard and unmovable. *Webster's* defines stony as "unfeeling; merciless, motionless or rigid, hardhearted and unfeeling, unemotional."[64]

We know Israel suffered all of these characteristics, but God had a better way for them to follow, a path to a new heart.

For me, getting a new heart not only gave me a new life physically, it also renewed me spiritually. I realize the miracle of my transplant and now can share the many ways God healed me, restored me, and grew me into who I am today. But the wait for this miracle was the most difficult wait I ever endured.

Richard Parrott writes, in a quarterly devotional, *Come Ye Apart*:

Waiting is part of life, including life in the Spirit.... "Stay" is not a pleasant command. We want to get on with it. Waiting time feels like wasting time to us.

But notice where the waiting is located—between "what my Father has promised" and "being clothed with power from on high." We wait between the promise and the power, between believing God will do it and knowing He has done it, between the prayer and the praise, between what the Bible says and what the Spirit says.

This is the spiritual train depot, with its hard seats, gray walls, and stone floor. The waiting area is silent, cold, and nondescript—and there's nothing you can do about it. Ah—could this be the purpose of waiting? Between the power and the promise, God wants us to stop "doing" and "be" still, "be" patient, "be" faithful. In your attitude of stillness, patience, and faithfulness, God will open your life to receive the promise of the power.

If you are waiting today, remember: the promise is good, the power will come.

Silently now I wait for Thee,
Ready, my God, Thy will to see.
Open my heart, illumine me,
Spirit divine.[65]

If you are willing to wait forever, chances are you won't have to wait long.

Throughout my illness, time and waiting were not a choice. Time was an affliction that taunted me in a contemptuous way.

I waited often for doctor's appointments that were scheduled weeks or months away when I felt I needed to see someone sooner.

I waited hours in the ER, with my husband propped up in a chair, leaning against the wall as he tried to rest his mind and body worn out from the frequent heart attack scares.

I watched the clock in my hospital room in anticipation of a transport employee coming with a stretcher to shuttle me to an operating room for a surgery or procedure.

How many days before I could go home, how many hours before I could see the doctor, how many weeks of chemo, how many days until I could receive a donor heart so I could stop counting how many days I may live?

Time never let me stop wondering until I learned to stop counting.

Four months after my transplant, an anticipated virus crept out of dormancy. My heart donor had CMV—cytomegalovirus—and it had spread throughout my bloodstream. For normal people, CMV is harmless. For someone with her immune system turned off, it could have been deadly.

The only form of treatment to make this virus go back into dormancy is an antiviral IV medicine similar to chemotherapy. I was admitted to the hospital as soon as the CMV was discovered and started on an IV treatment of this chemotherapy two times a day—every day. The treatments made me sick, but they were not near as bad as actual chemotherapy. When it was found that I could tolerate the medication, I was sent home on it for another month or so with nursing care.

I counted the six weeks on this regimen as a period of time I could tolerate and then be rid of, so I then could continue on my road to recovery. When it was done, I celebrated as the tubing was removed from my arm.

A week or two later, the virus reared its ugly head again. Once more I was admitted and started on the chemo treatments. This time, stronger doses were administered in hopes of the virus staying dormant. But after the prescribed treatment at home, it returned again. Testing was done to see if I was resistant to the medicine being used. I was. In fact, because the form of the virus I had (it has fifty-two strains) was resistant, it meant it would not respond to any of the medicines in the same category. It was time to try another course of something more powerful.

The only option left was a strong chemotherapy my heart transplant team had used only one time in twenty years. It would mean having the treatments two times a day for thirty days and in the hospital only, not at home. The medicine would make me very sick, they told me.

They were right.

Each treatment was preceded by an injection of Benadryl and a tranquilizer to prepare my body for the abusive chemical. As my heart surgeon put it, "It will be like having gasoline poured into your veins." The Benadryl was to help with the nausea and the tranquilizer was to help with the spasms and seizures the chemotherapy caused. The treatments were done during the day and at night, so by the time I recovered from one, the next treatment was being started.

Although the hospital did its best to accommodate me, thirty days locked in an isolation room with limited walks in the hallways and unbearable side effects made for a long time to be incarcerated.

Time ticked by steadily on the large clock on the drab hospital room wall. Often I was too sick to care, but sometimes I would lie on the bed, fighting the nausea and hoping for the final day to arrive. The days dragged on, meeting each other with the same routine and dread as the one before.

I thought about a lesson in endurance my mother-in-law, Rose, had taught me years before. I wanted to bake Christmas cookies with her and excitedly gathered all the ingredients and joined her in her kitchen. She offered plenty of skill and wisdom and we planned on baking the entire day.

One of the toppings I bought for the cookies were tiny, red cinnamon candies. After I arranged the ingredients on the kitchen table, I took the two-pound bag of them and tried to open it—carefully. But as I struggled to pull the plastic bag apart, it ripped, sending tiny round candies all over the linoleum floor.

"I'll get the broom," I lamented.

"Oh no!" insisted my mother-in-law. "You will get down on your hands and knees and pick up each one, carefully checking for dirt, and place them in this plastic bowl. When I was a little girl growing up in Brooklyn, my mother would buy a bag of lentils and we would have to sift through pounds of them and pick out all the little twigs and pebbles. Nothing was wasted or taken for granted. It taught all of us endurance and you are going to learn endurance now."

I got down on the floor and started picking up each little red pearl, thinking of her story and lesson—a good lesson for me to learn. It took time to pick through them and place them in the bowl. But when I was done, I was impressed with my small yet meaningful accomplishment. It was a lesson I will keep with me forever.

I endured day after day of treatment. When the chemotherapy was done after thirty grueling days, I was free finally to go home. I never wanted to go through that again and I knew it would take a while to recover from the side effects. I was discharged and the nurse called for a wheelchair to take me down to the entrance where John was waiting with the car.

"Oh, please let me walk down on my own," I begged the nurse. "I want to be as normal as possible."

I took my bag and walked to the elevators. When I emerged out of the front doors of the hospital lobby, the fresh air was wonderful and I relished it all the way home as the breeze from the car's open window blew on my face.

But shortly after my freedom was granted, the CMV virus came back once again. This was unheard of and my doctors searched for anything else they could do before they once again would have to imprison me to another bout of chemotherapy. They were not sure how much more my kidneys and body could take, and they were not sure how much I could take.

After much deliberation, I again was admitted for another month of torture. As I did before, I crossed off the days on the calendar hanging from my bulletin board. Once again, cards from friends and family decorated the room and my belongings took their place in the bedside dresser. Healthy snacks protruded from the top drawer and I stared at the dark TV screen, uninterested in its dribble of noise and irritating shows.

I kept busy, drawing with colored markers on the white poster board my friend Terry brought for me that was tacked to the wall. I read when I was able, worked on my computer when I could focus, and once again lamented for the end to come.

Time? There was lots of it, but I was trapped in a pallid time warp as, again, one day melded into another.

"God is extremely diligent and painfully slow," Chuck Swindoll touted one day while I was listening to his radio Bible study. His words were profound.

God always will complete what He needs to in our lives, but He will take as long as He needs to accomplish this completion of His will for us.

> I am going to send you what my Father has promised; but stay in the city until you have been clothed with power from on high.
> —Luke 24:49

"Stay… until you have been clothed with power from on high." If only we could all learn to stay and wait patiently, time no longer would be an enemy and the future would not have to be a fearful unknown.

The chemotherapy lasted another month and then I had to go home and remain on it for an additional six months. The news was more than I could bear.

By the time I finished the second round and went home to endure the additional six months, I had lost most of my hair, experienced terrible stomach problems, and felt like I was being poisoned. But I wanted to be "clothed with the power on high" God had promised. I determined to beat the poison and kept myself focused on God's will for my life.

I did as much as was physically possible at home, and sometimes got a ride to the ministry office where I worked, toting my chemotherapy in a backpack, hooking up the bag of medicine, and hanging it on the doorjamb in my office.

And I didn't stop living. Terry and I packed up the car one day and took the five-hour drive to Seattle to spend the day shopping and getting my mind off the torturous treatments. I hung the IV bottle from the visor in the front of the car and off we went. It was great to get out, and humorous to see the look on the teenager's face as she handed me my drink at the drive-through while the IV dripped into my arm.

While life can be full of painful times and difficult circumstances, God equips us to endure it with flair and get through the tough times unscathed. It is our choice. A quote by Tom Sobal, World Snowshoe Racing Champion, illustrates the benefit of painful endurance: "Pain is weakness leaving the body." And often the very pain that we fight to relieve ourselves of is the catalyst to make us stronger.

It took me a year to recover from the effects of this poisonous chemotherapy. And when I thought I was finally on the mend, another tragic accident put me back on the wheel of time. I broke my right leg in two places. It was bad. If I had moved the bone the wrong way it would have required surgery.

John and I had traveled to Florida for a family wedding. Mostly recovered from the months of chemo, I felt exuberated to leave town and enjoy the reception with friends and family.

On the last night of our trip, John and I and my sister and her fiancé walked the beach, illuminated by a bright, full moon. The ocean air was freeing and the sand between my toes soft and cool. The saltwater spray touched my face, gently caressing my skin. I loved it. I was free from the painful place my life had taken me.

We walked along a wooden fishing pier, jutted far out into the water. Waves splashed against the pilings and sprayed mist at the top rail. It was late, but people fished along the walkway under dim lighting: old men with buckets holding their precious catch; couples snuggled against the brisk wind, fishing lines hung into the dark ocean; and eager, young anglers hoping to catch bragging rights.

Afterward, we walked back to my sister's condo, passing through a bank parking lot. Lining the perimeter were native palm trees, their branches heavy with ripe coconuts.

"Oh, I want to bring some back home," I insisted.

My sister, tall and lanky, grabbed branches, pulling them low enough so I could amass an armful of coconuts.

"Look at me, stealing coconuts from the bank." I was joking as I stepped down from the sidewalk. Not watching where I placed my foot, I got my shoe stuck between the parking spot barrier and the curb, stopping me from taking the next step.

The armful of coconuts went flying and I jammed my right knee sideways. I never hit the ground, but collapsed from the pain. My tibia was fractured on both sides.

It's strange how a split second event can be remembered in slow motion. I knew as I went down that I had broken my leg, and the first thing I thought was *Oh, poor John,* knowing he would have to take care of me once more.

I also thought of the time I would have to be in a cast or wheelchair before I healed. It took fourteen weeks with no ability to walk on or use my right leg.

More counting.

More waiting for a chance to be free.

Time kept on ticking.

My leg is now healed, the chemotherapy is done, I am alive, and although time continues to propel me into the future, it is the present that really matters.

God will take care of the time He dominates.

Stay—until you have been clothed with power from on high.

Conclusion
What Is Your Heart Disease?

WHAT IS YOUR heart disease? Marriage? Finances? Children that have gone astray? Loss of a loved one? What do you choose to do with your situation?

I can't forget how I sunk to my knees when the Lord made clear what He was trying to say to Job: "Beware of turning to evil, which you seem to prefer to affliction" (36:21).

"Beware of turning to evil"—oh, those words struck me with powerful conviction. When afflicted with the pain of tragedy in life, it is easy to choose evil. Evil could be anger, bitterness, vengefulness, or the other side of the spectrum—apathy, lack of emotion or that numb lethargy that comes with shock. All these things are ways to avoid facing affliction head-on.

I quickly found out that avoiding the affliction of which I had grown weary caused me to choose evil. My moods and emotions became a whirlwind running out of control. But when I faced the pressure head-on and put my trust in the Lord, forging ahead to combat the pain, the result was empowering. If I was joyful in the face of affliction, people around me saw God's power. They could see the strength was not mine, but supernatural. God is given the glory. He is certainly made strong in our weakness.

But he said to me, "My grace is sufficient for you, for my power is made perfect in weakness." Therefore I will boast all the more gladly about my weaknesses, so that Christ's power may rest on me. That is why, for Christ's sake, I delight in weaknesses, in insults, in hardships, in persecutions, in difficulties. *For when I am weak, then I am strong.*
—2 Cor. 12:9-10, emphasis added

Often it seems the things we treasure most in our lives are what are taken away from us. Loss does much for breaking our hearts and our faith. The darkness of the enemy, as we know him, is supreme at hiding our treasures under his terror. But God never takes away what we treasure here on earth without revealing more treasure gained by the loss of the precious things to which we cleave:

I will go before you and make the rough places smooth; I will shatter the doors of bronze and cut through their iron bars. I will give you the treasures of darkness and hidden wealth of secret places, so that you may know that it is I, the LORD, the God of Israel, who calls you by your name.
—Isa. 45:2-3 NASB

Chuck Swindoll, in his Bible study guide *Hope in Hurtful Times*, lists three reasons for suffering:

That we might be prepared to comfort others.
That we might not trust in ourselves.
That we might learn to give thanks in everything.[66]

Jonah, an Old Testament writer, experienced these three concepts firsthand. After disobeying God, he was swallowed up by a great fish, vomited out on shore after three days in its belly, and then, after he completed his task in Nineveh, faced yet more despairing times:

Then the LORD God provided a vine and made it grow up over Jonah to give shade for his head to ease his discomfort, and Jonah was very happy about the vine. But at dawn the next day God provided a worm, which chewed the vine so that it withered. When the sun rose, God provided a scorching east wind, and the sun blazed on Jonah's head so that he grew faint. He wanted to die, and said, "It would be better for me to die than to live." But God said to Jonah, "Do you have a right to be angry about the vine?" "I do," he said. "I am angry enough to die." But the LORD said, "You have been concerned about this vine, though you did not tend it or make it grow. It sprang up overnight and died overnight. But Nineveh has more than a hundred and twenty thousand people who cannot tell their right hand from their left, and many cattle as well. Should I not be concerned about that great city?"

—Jonah 4:6-11

Jonah was self-absorbed. Instead of seeking the Lord for his strength, he looked to himself and found only anger. God tried to get his attention by allowing the vine to wither up. This was a small inconvenience compared to the people's needs in Nineveh. God's grace was there to sustain him, but he chose not to accept it.

The apostle Paul wrote much about pain, suffering, and heartache. But in all his writings, his drive is always towards grace.

Swindoll explains Paul's salutation found in 2 Corinthians 1:2:

Grace is ... God doing for us that which we don't deserve and cannot repay. And in its wake comes peace. Grace and peace don't come from ourselves—no matter how positive our thoughts; or from others—no matter how assuring their counsel. They come only from God.[67]

Everyday difficulties and personal hardships and pain can lead us to choose one of two paths. Either we allow these tremors to give birth to contaminating seeds of embitterment or we allow God to be the strength of our hearts and our portion forever.

Mike Webb of Mission Romania, a ministry based in Sierra Vista, Arizona, wrote:

It seems that there is in our hearts some little, locked, dark room full of foul, corrupting stuff that God means to get at and take care of. These areas are like little imps which enslave us and we are deceived into thinking we NEED them. Recognizing these "imps" is not enough for healing. There must be a decision of the will to tie them to the altar of God and let HIM destroy them with holy fire. Thus, our own private cremation.[68]

I recall a conversation I had with a friend's daughter as we ate lunch together. Misty, just eighteen years old, had suffered for years from an unknown illness. Plagued with weakness, headaches, stomach troubles, and other symptoms, she had become angry and bitter. Her hopelessness was evident in her expression of defeat.

"It's like I'm in the hurling of a hurricane," she said. "When will I get to the eye of the storm? I know there will be calm and rest there."

My reply was realistic. "It's actually a tornado! And the storm will not end until we reach heaven." Her look was disheartened and frustrated as she listened with disregard. I was trying to encourage her from my seasoned understanding of the will God has for each of our lives. He knows when we can be effective as Christians, and finding His will for our lives frees us to forge ahead without despair.

I know I can't keep looking back. The driving force in my life is to look ahead.

> Brethren, I do not count myself to have apprehended; but one thing I do, forgetting those things which are behind and reaching forward to those things which are ahead, I press toward the goal for the prize of the upward call of God in Christ Jesus.
> —Phil. 3:13-14 NKJV

John was by my side when the first open heart surgery almost took my life. The doctor called in the chaplain and prepared John for me to die. But I made it—again and again.

My cardiologist told me more than once I am the worst patient he ever has encountered—and he didn't mean my personality.

One new doctor was silent after sitting with me for two hours. She apologized and said she usually was not so quiet but she was dumbfounded at all that I had survived. Another doctor I saw—world famous—couldn't believe I was still alive.

I had much cause to worry—constantly. It took me a long time to actually get to a point where worry was a far-off threat that I could anticipate and stop before it became a problem.

One Sunday at church, the youth pastor shared his teaching on worry, based on Matthew 6:25-34. He asked the congregation a question: "Who here knows the secret to not worrying? If you do, please see me after the service."

I wanted to raise my hand with the answer when he asked his question. I don't think he expected anyone to approach him but if church hadn't been so crowded, I would have spoken to him after the service. I wanted to let him know I had reached a point where worry was only a distant fraction of my days. With all I had survived and had been through, how could I worry when God was always taking care of the things that could harm me? It was the same message of hope the prophet Jeremiah carried to the remnant exiled from Jerusalem to Babylon by Nebuchadnezzar: "For I know the plans I have for you,' declares the LORD, 'plans to prosper you and not to harm you, plans to give you hope and a future'" (Jer. 29:11). We, too, can stand on the same promise today. Yet fear and worry seem to be bred into us from birth.

When I was a young girl, I was terrified of thunderstorms, especially when they came during the night. I grew up with twelve siblings. The master bedroom was used as a dormitory for four of us. Our house was a three-level split so our bedrooms upstairs always stayed hot after a long summer day.

One day the summer heat forced us to keep two large windows in the bedroom open. We hoped for a breeze, but the air was still—a nighttime thunderstorm was on its way. The open screens exaggerated its fury. Although I slept with three siblings, violent storms turned our crowded room into a lonely, scary place.

Suddenly, the wind began to blow. Outside, the big oak tree's branches scraped against the house, creating shrilly screeches, while its leaves cast eerie shadows on the walls. I could smell the rain in the warm breeze coming through the windows and hear the distant thunder approaching.

In anticipation of the storm's arrival, I pulled my blanket over my head, leaving a thin slit over my eyes so I could keep watch for lightning.

I imagined horrible destruction from lightning strikes or the oak tree coming down on the roof. I always feared the silent darkness of a power outage.

Thunder shook the house and lightning flashed across the walls, illuminating every corner. I curled up deeper under my protective covering.

How I trembled under that quilt, my body becoming drenched with sweat! I dared not emerge from the protection of my cocoon until I was sure the storm had moved past.

Finally, it stopped. When I knew I was safe, I threw off the covers and the cool, fresh air, sweetened from the rain, breathed relief on my entire body.

Worry is the storm we need not fear. It is the heavy, moist air trapped under the blanket of concern.

With all I have been through, worry no longer can entrap me. I am thankful to be alive. Yes, I am.

I am thankful I am not living in a third world country because I would be dead.

I am thankful my husband is a man of God and has stuck by me in all the lonely and painful hours.

I am thankful I can walk and drive and get around.

There are so many things for which to be thankful. But if I look at the list, none of them are eternal.

> But all of you who held fast to the Lord your God are still alive today.
>
> —Deut. 4:4

The one thing on which I meditate each day is being thankful for my faith in a God who is bigger than any trial I will face. I don't pray with an agenda and I hardly pray for healing anymore. Instead, I pray I will be faithful and worthy to be a witness of God's power. This is much bigger than healing.

Many times I have had people offer suggestions for why I am sick and have not been healed. One friend said, "If you had cancer, you'd either be better by now or dead."

How do I continue to endure and still give thanks? I hold onto God's Word, I pray always, and I surrender everything to God. Remember what the Lord spoke to me earlier? "I cannot heal you until you are ready to accept how I choose to heal you—and I am not finished yet." I must surrender all I am to Him and trust Him. Remember the anchors God gave me to hold on in the storms?

> Beware of turning to evil, which you seem to prefer to affliction.
> —Job 36:21

> Do not grieve, for the joy of the LORD is your strength.
> —Neh. 8:10

> Deal courageously, and the LORD shall be with the good.
> —2 Chron. 19:11 KJV

Nancy DeMoss, in her daily radio program encourages us to be thankful:

> Sometimes it's really hard to give thanks. Sometimes it's costly to give thanks. Sometimes you have to offer a sacrifice of thanksgiving—through your tears—to say:

> Lord, though I do not understand why You would have me go through these circumstances—though I do not understand why I am receiving these divorce papers that I don't want, I don't understand why my son or daughter is responding in these ways that are not pleasing to You—I choose in the midst of this struggle, in the midst of this pressure, and in the midst of these problems to give You thanks because You are still God. And You are still good and You are accomplishing Your purposes through every circumstance that is in my life.[69]

Each day brings me one more opportunity to make a difference. Maybe something I do or say can bring encouragement to someone else in a heart-wrenching situation. I deal with a physically broken heart, but that does not mean I do not also deal with emotional and spiritual brokenness. My dreadful medical problems may have physically damaged my heart that carries the life-blood through my body, but the soul God made in me resides in my spiritual heart. It is in this spiritual heart that I really carry the life God is interested in.

David Wilkerson writes, in his *Pulpit Series Newsletter*:

Right now, you may be going through the hardest time you've ever faced. Your life may be unsettled, and things may look hopeless. Could it be a lost job? Maybe your financial situation is out of control. There seems to be no way out for you. Every avenue to which you turn fills you with more stress, confusion, and weariness.

That is when the mind begins to reason, "How can I have peace with all this debt hanging over my head? How can I possibly be calm when I need a financial miracle? I'm at the end of my rope. The future seems so uncertain."

Maybe your family is in a crisis, your marriage is struggling, or your health is failing, and there seems to be no hope ahead. You tell yourself, "If I just could see some light at the end of the tunnel. Yet all I see is uncertainty on all sides. If I just could get healing for my body (deliverance for my child, out of debt) then I'd have peace. Give me a miracle, and I'll know peace."

When Christ promised the disciples His peace, it was as if He was saying to them (as well as to us today): "I know you don't understand the hard times you face. You don't comprehend the Cross and the suffering I am about to face. Yes, you are about to be tried beyond your human capacity to endure. You're going to be confused and feel forsaken by the Father."

It doesn't matter what you're going through. Your life might look like it has been struck by a tornado. You might endure trials that cause others to look at you as a modern-day Job. But in the midst of your troubles, when you call on the Holy Spirit to baptize you in the peace of Christ, He will do it.

People might point to you and say, "That person's world has come completely apart. Yet he's determined to trust God's Word, live or die. How can he do it? How does he go on? He should have quit long ago. Yet he hasn't given up. And through it all, he hasn't compromised anything he believes. What amazing peace! It's beyond understanding."[70]

This book really has no ending. My life, as many days as I have left here on earth, will continue regardless of how much I learn or how much closer I grow to the Lord. The tornado of trials will remain, hurling around me, and the same power that allows turmoil and tribulation in my life will carry me closer and closer to heaven.

My physical heart was failing until I received new life from Danielle—my angel on earth. More essential is the health of my spiritual heart, which received new life through Christ.

A heart like mine must find God's will for my life. Your heart also must navigate the path and process to bring you to His will and purpose for your life.

WHERE TO FIND CINDY AND MORE INFORMATION ABOUT HER ON THE WEB:

Website:
http://www.aHeartLikeMine.com
http://www.cindyscinto.com

Blog:
http://www.cindyscinto.blogspot.com

MySpace:
http://www.myspace.com/lovelifetogo

Facebook:
http://www.facebook.com/cindy.scinto

Twitter:
http://twitter.com/aheartlikemine

Please post feedback about this book to:
http://www.cindyscinto.com/contact_me.html

Not online?
Cindy Scinto
P.O. Box 863
Spokane Valley, WA 99016-0863

Watch for Cindy's next two books in the *Heart Like Mine* series: *A Heart Like Yours, Understanding God's Will for Your Life* and *A Heart Like His, Living God's Will for Your Life*

Glossary

Edited by Heart Transplant Coordinator Pam Holland, RN, BSN, CCTC

The following are terms used in cardiology and similar medical fields. I have prepared this glossary to be as accurate as possible but have modified some of the definitions to relate to the layman in all of us. Do not use this glossary for a medical diagnosis or as a replacement for a medical doctor's assessment. This information is provided for reference only.

A

ablation – Ablation is used to treat abnormal heart rhythms. Nonsurgical ablation, used for many types of arrhythmias, is performed in a special lab called the electrophysiology (EP) laboratory. Catheter ablation is a procedure that is used to destroy (ablate) areas of the heart which are causing arrhythmias. In a radiofrequency ablation, electrophysiologists pinpoint the area and then use radio wave energy to "cauterize" the tiny part of the heart muscle causing the abnormal heart rhythm. Catheter ablation plays an important role in the management of most types of cardiac arrhythmias.

abnormal heart rhythm – see *arrhythmia*

acute coronary artery disease – Acute coronary artery disease is chest pain and other symptoms that happen because the heart does not get enough blood. It includes unstable angina and heart attack. Acute coronary syndrome happens because plaque narrows or blocks the arteries that supply blood to the heart. Most of these arteries lie on the outside of the heart, (a muscle) providing the blood flow muscle needs to function. Plaque is made of cholesterol and other things. Over time, plaque can build up in the arteries. This is known as coronary artery disease.

adrenaline (epinephrine) – One of the body's many hormones is adrenaline. Higher amounts of the hormone epinephrine (adrenaline) in blood in early morning can lead to increased risk for heart attack.

angiogenesis – Angiogenesis occurs naturally in the body and involves the growth of new blood vessels. Coronary artery disease, peripheral artery disease, and stroke cause insufficient blood supply and oxygen to tissues and causes the body to grow additional vessels. The body's first response to less blood flow to the heart is to grow these tiny new "collateral" vessels increase blood flow around a blockage. In some people, the process stops or does not supply enough new vessels. Proteins in the body can help trigger new blood vessel growth and increase oxygen supply to the ischemic tissue. Angiogenic proteins are referred to as vascular endothelial growth factor (VEGF) and fibroblast growth factor (FGF).

AMA – "Against Medical Advice," meaning a patient has made a decision that is deemed medically unsound by the physician, such as signing yourself out of the hospital before recommendation.

angiogram – see *catheterization*

angioplasty – A procedure in which the narrowing in the lumen of a blood vessel is treated by inflating a balloon attached to the tip of a catheter and running it up through the femur artery with a catheter wire.

arrhythmia – An irregular heartbeat is an arrhythmia (also called *dysrhythmia*). Heart rates can sometimes be irregular. A heart rate of fifty to one hundred beats per minute is normal. Arrhythmias can occur with normal, fast, or slow heart rates. Slow heart rates are called *bradyarrhythmias* and are less than sixty beats per minute. Fast heart rates are called *tachyarrhythmias* and are faster than one hundred beats per minute.

B

ballooning – With simple angioplasty, a balloon at the end of a long tube is threaded through an artery in the groin. The doctor guides the tube up the artery and into the heart, inflating the balloon where the vessel has narrowed. The balloon opens up the vessel's walls. Then it is deflated and removed.

blockage – If there is too much cholesterol in the bloodstream, the excess may be deposited in arteries, including the coronary (heart) arteries, where it contributes to the narrowing and blockages that cause the signs and symptoms of heart disease.

blood pressure – The force exerted by the blood on the walls of the coronary arteries is a person's blood pressure. Pressure can be measured at the wrist and other points where arteries are near the surface of the body. Blood pressure is measured with two numbers: systolic (the top number in a reading) and diastolic (the bottom number). It is measured in millimeters of mercury (abbreviated mm Hg) using a device called a sphygmomanometer. Systolic pressure refers to the force of blood against the walls of the arteries when the heart contracts to pump blood to the rest of the body. Diastolic pressure refers to the pressure within the arteries as the heart relaxes and refills with blood (which explains why the diastolic number is always lower than the systolic measurement).

blood transfusion – The transfer of blood from one person to another. Transfusions are performed to replace a substantial loss of blood and as supportive treatment in certain diseases and blood disorders.

bone density – Bone density tests (also called *bone mineral density tests* or *bone scans*) evaluate the strength of your bones by measuring a small part of one or a few bones. Knowing the strength of your bones can help your doctor recommend prevention steps and osteoporosis medication, if needed, to prevent bone loss and fractures.

brachytherapy – Stents are used in arteries and are very effective at keeping blood vessels along the heart open. But stents can block back up in 20 percent of people. This renarrowing is called *in-stent restenosis*. Restenosis can be caused by scar tissue that forms in when the stent was implanted. Some scar tissue is useful as it covers the metal stent and helps prevent blood clots from forming. But in some patients, the process does not stop, and the scar tissue blocks the stent. When restenosis occurs, doctors can fix the blockage by radiating the stent. This is called *brachytherapy*.

bpm – Beats per minute; used to define heart rate

bypass surgery – During coronary artery bypass graft surgery (also called *CABG*, spoken as "cabbage"), a blood vessel is removed or redirected from one area of the body and placed around the area or areas of narrowing to "bypass" the blockages and restore blood flow to the heart muscle. This vessel is called a *graft*. These substitute blood vessels can come from your chest, legs, or arms. They're safe to use because there are other pathways that take blood to and from those tissues. The surgeon will decide which graft(s) to use depending on the location of your blockage, the amount of blockage, and the size of your coronary arteries.

C

cardiologist – A specialized doctor who treats conditions related to the heart cardiopulmonary arrest – see *heart attack*

cartilage – A tough, elastic, fibrous connective tissue found in various parts of the body, such as the joints

catheter – A flexible or rigid hollow tube employed to drain fluids from body cavities or to distend body passages

catheterization – A catheter is inserted into the femoral artery and threaded to the blockage. The doctor will follow the path of the catheter through an X-ray and will perform balloon dilation in the area. This is typically followed by stenting which is catheter-based placement of metal mesh expandable cylindrical scaffolding (called a "stent") that keeps the diseased artery open to its normal size. This is performed when angioplasty alone cannot dilate the artery sufficiently or in certain locations where stents works better than angioplasty alone.

catheterization wire – During a heart catheterization, a thin, flexible tube called a *catheter* (or *wire*) is threaded through a blood vessel in the groin, or sometimes in the wrist. This wire is guided up into the heart. The doctor can measure pressures, take blood samples, and inject a special dye (contrast material) into the coronary arteries of the heart. The dye's movement through the heart's chambers and blood vessels allows the doctor to see areas of blockage.

centrifugal machine – A blood centrifuge uses the manageable force of gravity to separate blood's components by spinning it at a high speed.

chemotherapy – Chemotherapy is the general term for any treatment involving the use of chemical agents to stop cancer cells from growing. Chemotherapy is designed to kill cancer cells. It can be administered through a vein, injected into a body cavity, or delivered orally in the form of a pill, depending on which drug is used.

clinical trial – In health care, clinical trials are conducted to allow safety and efficacy data to be collected for new drugs or devices. These can take place only when satisfactory information has been gathered on the product's quality and its nonclinical safety. Depending on the type of product and the stage of its development, clinical trials initially enroll healthy volunteers and/or patients into small studies, followed by larger scale studies in patients that often compare the new product with the currently prescribed treatment. As positive safety data are gathered, the number of patients can be increased. The Food and Drug Administration (FDA) determines if a new product is safe and either approves or disproves it for manufacturing.

code blue – Often the term *code* is used as slang for a cardiopulmonary arrest happening to a patient in a hospital or clinic, requiring a team of providers (sometimes called a *code team*) to rush to the specific location and begin immediate resuscitative efforts. Every hospital or clinic has its own system for disseminating information about emergencies, and many use the term *code* plus a color or number to signify exactly what kind of emergency is occurring. *Code Blue* is often used to refer to a cardiopulmonary arrest.

coding – Going into cardiopulmonary arrest

congenital – Of or pertaining to a condition present at birth, whether inherited or caused by the environment, especially the uterine environment.[71]

coronary – Encircling in the manner of a crown; in cardiology this refers to the heart's arteries and, by extension, to related diseases, defects, or malfunctions of the heart

coronary artery - Coronary arteries supply blood to the heart muscle. Like all other tissues in the body, the heart muscle needs oxygen-rich blood to function, and oxygen-depleted blood must be carried away. The coronary arteries consist of two main arteries: the right and left coronary arteries, and their two branches, the circumflex artery and the left anterior descending artery.

coronary spasms – Plaque is not always the cause of a heart attack. In some cases, the coronary artery spasms and contracts, obstructing blood flow and causing chest pain. Blood clots form more easily on arterial walls roughened by plaque deposits and may block one or more of the narrowed coronary arteries completely and cause a heart attack. Arteries may also narrow suddenly as a result of an arterial spasm. (Spasms are most commonly triggered by smoking.) Cold weather, emotional stress, and other factors can cause these spasms. But in many other cases, it is not known what triggers them. These spasms cause angina, chest pain, and discomfort.

coronary vessel – Coronary circulation is the circulation of blood in the blood vessels that supply blood to and from the heart muscle itself. Although blood fills the heart's chambers, the heart's muscle tissue, or myocardium, is so thick that it requires coronary blood vessels to deliver blood deep into it. The vessels that deliver oxygen-rich blood to the myocardium are known as *coronary arteries*.

CT scan – Computed tomography (CT) scanning is performed by taking high resolution X-ray images using a multi-slice scanner. This advanced imaging can detect coronary artery disease, evaluate congenital heart disease, and may be used to evaluate a patient's heart prior to a complex catheter ablation procedure.

CMV – Cytomegalovirus, or CMV, is found universally throughout all geographic locations and socioeconomic groups, and infects between 50 percent and 85 percent of adults in the United States by forty years of age. Once a person becomes infected, the virus remains alive, but usually dormant, within that person's body for life. Recurrent disease rarely occurs unless the person's immune system is suppressed due to therapeutic drugs or disease. Therefore, for the vast majority of people CMV infection is not a serious problem. However, infection with CMV is a major cause of disease and death in immune-compromised patients, including organ transplant recipients, patients with cancer, patients receiving immunosuppressive drugs, and HIV-infected patients.

D

depression – Depression is a serious medical illness that involves the brain. It's more than just a feeling of being "down in the dumps" or "blue" for a few days. For the more than twenty million people in the United States who have depression, the feelings do not go away. They persist and interfere with everyday life. Symptoms can include sadness, loss of interest or pleasure in activities one used to enjoy, change in weight, difficulty sleeping or oversleeping, energy loss, feelings of worthlessness, and thoughts of death or suicide.[72]

diagonal artery – Smaller branch of the coronary artery

double bypass surgery – Coronary artery bypass surgery, also called *coronary artery bypass graft surgery*, and colloquially *heart bypass* or *bypass surgery*, is a surgical procedure performed to relieve angina and reduce the risk of death from coronary artery disease. The terms *single bypass, double bypass, triple bypass, quadruple bypass*, and *quintuple bypass* refer to the number of coronary arteries bypassed in the procedure. In other words, a double bypass means two coronary arteries are bypassed.

E

Echocardiogram – An echocardiogram (also called an *echo*) is a non-invasive painless test that allows cardiologists to see if your heart is functioning normally or if it is enlarged, weakened or has a damaged valve. Ultrasound waves are directed through the chest to the heart. The echoes of the sound waves are processed and used to produce images of the heart.

EKG/ECG – An electrocardiogram (ECG) is a simple test that traces the electrical activity of your heart. During an ECG, you lie flat on a table, connected to an ECG machine with wires taped to your chest, arms, and legs. The test is painless and takes only a few minutes. The ECG produces a printout that doctors can examine to diagnose arrhythmias or other types of heart disease.

electrical pathways – The flow of electricity within the heart. The heart's electrical system causes the heart to beat, controls the heart rate (the number of beats per minute), and has special pathways (conduction pathways) that carry the electrical signals throughout the lower heart chambers (ventricles) for each heartbeat. The electrical chain reaction that occurs in the heart is much like ripples on the calm surface of a pond.

electromagnetic field – The field of force associated with electric charge in motion, having both electric and magnetic components and containing a definite amount of electromagnetic energy. Magnetic fields can interrupt the proper functioning of a pacemaker.

electrophysiological cardiologist – These physicians have special training in the diagnosis and treatment of cardiac rhythm abnormalities. Electrophysiology is the study of cardiac arrhythmias, or abnormal heart rhythms.

electrophysiology – An electrophysiology (EP) study is a test that records the heart's electrical activity and electrical pathways. This test is used to help determine the cause of heart rhythm disturbances.

elevated pressure – Or known as hypertension, is characterized by a persistent increase in the force that the blood exerts upon the walls of the arteries. It is normal for this force to increase with stress or physical exertion, but with hypertension, the patient's blood pressure is high even at rest.

Hypertension is defined as systolic pressure greater than 140 mm Hg or diastolic pressure greater than 90 mm Hg; optimal blood pressure is less than 120/80 mm Hg.

Some 60 million Americans have hypertension, but only about half of them know it, primarily because it so rarely causes any noticeable symptoms and is usually detected only incidentally during a routine physical examination. But left untreated, hypertension promotes atherosclerosis (narrowing of the arteries) and increases the risk of heart attack, stroke, kidney damage and destruction of tiny blood vessels in the eye, which can result in vision loss. For these reasons hypertension is often called "the silent killer."

Fortunately, if detected early and treated properly, the prognosis is good.

epinephrine – Epinephrine (see *adrenaline*) is a hormone.

F

femur artery – A large artery that starts in the lower abdomen and goes down into the thigh. It is the main artery of the thigh, supplying blood to the groin and lower extremities.

FGF-1 – Fibroblast growth factors, or FGFs, are a family of growth factors involved in angiogenesis, wound healing, and embryonic development.

full metal jacket – [medical slang] In terms of the heart's coronary arteries, this means that metal stents have been placed in the entire artery, lining it completely.

H

heart attack – A heart attack occurs when blood flow to the heart is blocked. Without blood and the oxygen it carries, part of the heart muscle starts to die. It's also called a *myocardial infarction*, or MI. Heart attacks happen when blood flow to the heart is blocked. This usually occurs because fatty deposits called *plaque* have built up inside the coronary arteries that supply blood to the heart. If a plaque breaks open, the body tries to fix it by forming a clot around it. Some heart attacks are sudden but most heart attacks start slowly with mild pain or discomfort.

heart catheterization – see *catheterization*

hostel – An inexpensive, supervised lodging place for young people on bicycle trips, hikes, educational trips, etc.

HRV – Heart rate variability (HRV) refers to the beat-to-beat alterations in heart rate.

Hypertension is defined as systolic pressure greater than 140 mm Hg or diastolic pressure greater than 90 mm Hg; optimal blood pressure is less than 120/80 mm Hg.

I

intervention – Also known as *angioplasty* or *percutaneous coronary intervention*

IV – An intravenous (inside the vein) device for delivering electrolyte solutions, medicines, and nutrients

immune system – In simplest terms, the immune system is a balanced network of cells and organs that work together to defend you against disease. It blocks foreign proteins from getting into your body. If a few happen to sneak by your biological sentry, not to worry. With a powerful "search and destroy" task force, your body deploys a host of additional immune cell forces designed to hunt down these unwanted invaders and ultimately work to destroy them.

immune compromised – A state in which the immune system's ability to fight infectious disease is compromised or entirely absent. Most cases of immunodeficiency are acquired ("secondary") but some people are born with defects in the immune system, or primary immunodeficiency. Transplant patients take medications to suppress their immune system as an anti-rejection measure. A person who has an immunodeficiency of any kind is said to be *immunocompromised*. An immunocompromised person may be particularly vulnerable to opportunistic infections in addition to normal infections that could affect everyone.

L

left anterior descending artery – The left anterior descending artery branches off the left coronary artery and supplies blood to the front of the heart.

lethargic – Sluggish, drowsy, tired

Lou Gehrig's Disease – Amyotrophic lateral sclerosis (ALS), commonly known as Lou Gehrig's disease, is a progressive neuromuscular disease.

ALS is characterized by a progressive degeneration of motor nerve cells in the brain (upper motor neurons) and spinal cord (lower motor neurons). When the motor neurons can no longer send impulses to the muscles, the muscles begin to waste away (atrophy), causing increased muscle weakness.

ALS does not affect or impair a person's intellectual reasoning, vision, hearing or sense of taste, smell, and touch.

ALS is often referred to as a syndrome because the disease becomes apparent in various patterns. ALS occurs rarely and spontaneously. Currently, there is no cure for amyotrophic lateral sclerosis.

N

Nitroglycerin – "Nitro" is a vasodilator, a medicine that opens blood vessels to improve blood flow. It is used to treat angina, a type of chest pain, that happens when there is not enough blood flowing to the heart. To improve blood flow to the heart, nitroglycerin opens up (dilates) the arteries in the heart (coronary arteries), which improves symptoms and reduces how hard the heart has to work.

NPO – Commonly used in the hospital, meaning no food or drink allowed

nuclear stress test – Stress Test (usually with ECG; also called treadmill or exercise ECG) A test that is given while a patient walks on a treadmill or pedals a stationary bike to monitor the heart during exercise. Breathing and blood pressure rates are also monitored. A stress test may be used to detect coronary artery disease, and/or to determine safe levels of exercise following a heart attack or heart surgery.

O

occlusion – A coronary occlusion is the partial or complete obstruction of blood flow in a coronary artery. This condition may cause a heart attack. In some patients coronary occlusion causes only mild pain, tightness, or vague discomfort that could be ignored. However, the myocardium is damaged.

oncology – The branch of medical science dealing with tumors, including the origin, development, diagnosis, and treatment of cancer

open-heart surgery – Open-heart surgery is done while the bloodstream is diverted through a heart-lung machine. Some of the different types of open-heart surgeries are valve replacements, coronary bypass, and heart transplants.

P

pacemaker – A pacemaker is an electronic device used to treat patients who have symptoms caused by abnormally slow heartbeats. A pacemaker is capable of keeping track of the patient's heartbeats. If the patient's heart is beating too slowly, the pacemaker will generate electrical signals similar to the heart's natural signals, causing the heart to beat faster. The purpose of the pacemaker is to maintain heartbeats so that adequate oxygen and nutrients are delivered through the blood to the organs of the body.

pacemaker dependent – Heavily or totally dependent on a pacemaker to keep your heart beating

pharmacological – The science dealing with the preparation, uses, and especially the effects of drugs

plaque – Cardiovascular arterial disease is a narrowing of the coronary arteries, the vessels that supply blood to the heart muscle, generally due to the buildup of plaques in the arterial walls, a process known as atherosclerosis. Plaques are composed of cholesterol-rich fatty deposits, collagen, other proteins, and excess smooth muscle cells. Atherosclerosis, which usually progresses very gradually over a lifetime, thickens and narrows the arterial walls, impeding the flow of blood and starving the heart of the oxygen and vital nutrients it needs (also called "ischemia"). This can cause muscle cramp-like chest pain called angina.

psychologist – A person trained and educated to perform psychological research, testing, and therapy. Psychologists study the physical, cognitive, emotional, and social aspects of behavior, and provide mental health care in hospitals, clinics, schools, and private practices.

physiologically – Being in accord with or characteristic of the normal functioning of a living organism

PVC – Or *premature ventricular complex*. This electrical impulse starts in the ventricle, causing the heart to beat earlier than expected. Usually, the heart returns to its normal rhythm right away.

R

restenosis – When an artery or stent collapses or closes off rotablation – A nonsurgical technique for treating diseased arteries in which a special catheter with a diamond-coated tip is guided to the point of narrowing in the artery. It then spins at high speeds, and grinds away the blockage or plaque on the artery walls. It is not safe to rotablate a coronary vessel more then a few times.

S

stent – A stent is a wire mesh stainless steel tube that holds an artery open and keeps it from closing again. It becomes a permanent part of your artery.

Fatty deposits can block blood flow through arteries and cause pain. A piece may break off, form a clot, and cause a heart attack or stroke. A stent opens the blockage and keeps it open, which allows blood to flow smoothly. Good blood flow reduces pain and risks of clots forming.

The doctor will insert a tiny, flexible plastic tube called a catheter through an artery in our groin, leg, or arm. A special dye is injected so blood flow through the arteries is visible on the TV monitors. The doctor moves a balloon catheter, and then a stent, to the site of the blockage. The balloon is inflated and stretched wide against the artery walls, which opens the blockage. Then the balloon is deflated and taken out, leaving the stent in place.

sternum – The sternum is a long, flat bone located in the center of the chest. It connects to the rib bones via cartilage, forming the rib cage with them, and thus helps to protect the lungs, heart, and major blood vessels from physical trauma. The sternum is sometimes cut open to gain access to the thoracic contents when performing cardiothoracic surgery.

stroke – A stroke, sometimes called a "brain attack," occurs when blood flow to an area in the brain is cut off. As a result, the brain cells, deprived of the oxygen and glucose needed to survive, die. If not caught early, permanent brain damage can result.

T

tachycardia – A rapid heart rate, usually defined as greater than one hundred beats per minute

U

underdeployed – This is when a stent is not fully expanded, leaving a small "pocket" or space between the stent and the wall of the artery. This is dangerous as it can cause restenosis and movement in the artery.

V

VAD – A *ventricular assist device* is a mechanical pump that helps a weakened heart pump blood throughout the body. It is used as a "bridge-to-transplant" for those who are hospitalized with heart failure and waiting for a donor heart to be available.

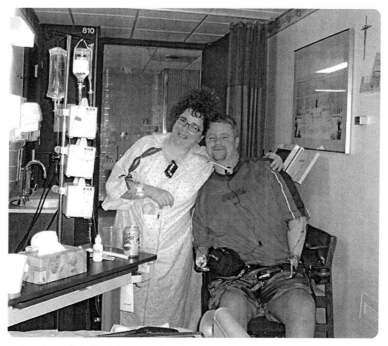

Cindy and Jeff visitng while she was in the hospital waiting for a life-saving heart transplant.

Cindy and her husband, John, 3 years after her heart transplant, enjoying a trip to California.

Her faithful
canine, Jackson.

Cindy's son, Jonathan.
Always an encourager!

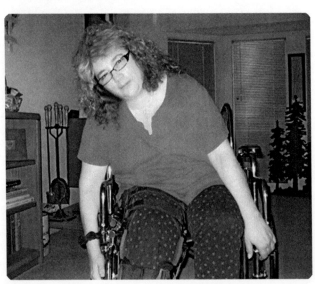

Wheelchair confinement after breaking her leg in Florida.
Fourteen weeks of waiting … all for an armful of coconuts!

Dr. Sandler, Cindy, and Dr. Icenogle

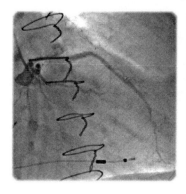

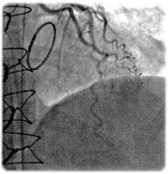

My heart before the transplant. There are hardly any blood vessels visible. Dye cannot run through blocked areas. The wire at the bottom is from a pacemaker. The twisted ties are metal wires holding my rib cage together.

After the transplant. You can see the plentiful blood vessels filled with dye indicating good circulation. The oval shape in the upper left hand corner is the annuplasty ring in the mitral valve. Danielle's heart is strong and healthy.

Cindy with Don Harter of Executive Flight, Inc.

Cindy got to meet the man responsible for flying her transplanted heart from Seattle to Spokane. Don Harter, Chief Operations Officer for Executive Flight, Inc., wanted to give back. He flew the first donor heart by Lear jet in 1983. "It brings tears to my eyes," Harter comments.

Don drag races with Hart Breaker Racing. His car sports the Donate Life Today! logo to promote organ donation awareness.

Executive Flight, Inc.
www.execflight.com

http://www.HartBrakerRacing.com

go red in your own fashion.

go red, anyway you want... eat red - **apples, cherries, tomatoes,** leave red **kisses** on someone's cheek. laugh so hard your **face** turns red. but whatever you do, do it for **your heart**. take a moment everyday and put your hand on your heart, and then make your own promise to be **heart healthy**.

Go **Red** for women

American Heart Association

Learn and Live

www.goredforwomen.org
1-888-MY HEART

If you are reading this ad,

you are at **risk.**

Fact is, everyone's potentially at risk for heart disease and stroke. The good news is even small changes in your lifestyle can help you live a longer, healthier life. That's why it's important to understand your risk factors — traits and lifestyle habits that increase your risk — and manage the ones you can control. We can help you can. Visit us online at **American Heart.org** or call **1-800-AHA-USA-1**.

POWER TO END STROKE.℠
You are the Power

American Heart | American Stroke
Association₀ | Association₀
Learn and Live₀

Risk factors you can control:
* High Blood Pressure
* Tobacco Smoke
* High Blood Cholesterol
* Physical Activity
* Obesity
* Diabetes

Risk factors you can't control:
* Increasing Age
* Sex (gender)
* Race
* Family Medical History
* Previous Heart Attack
  or Stroke

We have information to help you identify and manage your risk factors. Contact us and take the first step towards preventing a heart attack or stroke.

Natassia gives blood to feel like
she's making a difference.

Josh is living proof
that she is.

Donate blood today and change a life, starting with your own.
Call 1-800-GIVE LIFE or visit givelife.org

**American
Red Cross**

H20396

 **®** Organ, eye, and tissue donation can offer those waiting for a transplant, a new chance at healthy, productive, and normal lives.

- 100,000 people in the United States are waiting for a life-saving organ transplant.
- Sadly, 18 people die each day waiting for a transplant.
- One donor can save or enhance the lives of over 50 people.

You can help by registering your donation wishes today!

Visit **www.donatelife.net** to find out how to register in your state.

To ensure your family and friends know your donation wishes, talk to them about your decision.

It's about living. It's about life!

Endnotes

Introduction

1. David Swartz *Dancing with Broken Bones*. 1985, © David Swartz. Permission granted by the author. 41.

Chapter One

2. "If I Only Had a Heart," Metro-Goldwyn-Mayer, 1939.
3. The medical center where my transplant was performed, Sacred Heart Medical Center in Spokane, Washington, boasts the highest success rates for patients surviving a heart transplant at the one-year tally and the three-year tally. According to an article published by *The Living Legacy Foundation* in Seattle, Washington:

    The program ... began in 1989 [and] now posts survival rates that routinely exceed national levels," said Dr. Timothy Icenogle, the 54-year-old cardiac surgeon who directs the program.

    Only one of thirty-two patients died after receiving heart transplants at Sacred Heart between January 2003 and June 2005, according to data released last month from a national transplant registry.

    That's a success rate of nearly 97 percent after one year, compared with nearly 88 percent nationwide, and more than 95 percent after three years, compared with less than 80 percent nationally, according to the Scientific Registry of Transplant Recipients (SRTR).

Not only was I in a place where the survival rates are the highest, but my surgeon is a man who looks to the Lord for his ability to save lives:

"I don't believe in the providence of luck," Icenogle said. "I believe in mathematical probability and the providence of the Lord."

Excerpted from "Heartfelt Gift" by Jonel Aleccia, The Spokesman-Review, February 14, 2007 Copyright 2007 by The Spokesman-Review. Used by permission.

4. Hues Corporation. "Rock the Boat." 1974.
5. Bryan Duncan. "A Heart Like Mine." Myrrh, 1999.
6. Taken from *My Utmost for His Highest* by Oswald Chambers, edited by James Reimann, © 1992 by Oswald Chambers Publications Assn., Ltd., and used by permission of Discovery House Publishers, Grand Rapids MI 49501. All rights reserved, February 27.
7. Dr. Mimi Guarneri, M.D., FACC. *The Heart Speaks*. New York: Touchstone, 2007, 158.
8. Guarneri, 102.
9. Reprinted by permission. *Waking the Dead*, John Eldredge, November 14, 2006, Thomas Nelson, Inc. Nashville, Tennessee. All rights reserved.
10. Ilan Wittstein, M.D., Hopkins cardiologist. Johns Hopkins Medicine, February 9, 2005. April 2008 http://www.hopkinsmedicine.org/Press_releases/2005/02_10_05.html.

Chapter Two
11. Lewis Carroll. *Alice's Adventures in Wonderland*. 1865.
12. University of Washington Television. January 2008, http://www.uwtv.org/newsletter/insider_1207.asp.
13. Ibid.
14. November 2007, Public Citizen. http://www.citizen.org/documents/FCT-Why_Doctors_Practice_Where_04-05-04.pdf.

15. Guarneri, 65-79.

16. Guarneri, 122.

17. Charles R. Swindoll. *Hope in Hurtful Times: A Study of 1 Peter.* California: Insight for Living, 1990, 50.

18. Ibid, 53.

19. "vapor." Merriam-Webster Online Dictionary. 2009.Merriam-Webster Online. 12 August 2009 <http://www.merriam-webster.com/dictionary/vapor>.

20. Excerpted from "She Needs a Christmas Miracle," The Spokesman-Review, December 8, 2003. Copyright 2003 The Spokesman-Review, used by permission.

21. Susan Gvozdas. "She's Too Well." *Central Penn Business Journal.* Harrisburg, PA. March 2004.

22. Thomas Stegmann Professor, M.D. "Article Being Submitted for Publication." May 2008.

23. Joni Eareckson Tada. *Joni.* New York: Bantam, 1978, 116.

24. Jill Briscoe. *Faith Enough to Finish.* Illinois: Tyndale House Publishers, 2001, 170.

Chapter Three

25. Mark Farner., audiocassette. "Isn't It Amazing." Just Another Injustice, Royal Tapestry Music, 1988.

26. Cindy Mah. "Mah's Matters." Taken from a newsletter to her family. 2005. Her husband is battling stage-two colon cancer.

27. Nicole E. Squibbs. "Duck shot by arrow is recovering." *Yuma Daily Sun*, May 19, 2007, http://www.yumasun.com/news/duck_34132___article.html/arrow_haugo.html.

28. Phillip Keller. *A Shepherd Looks at Psalm 23.* Michigan: Daybreak Books, 1970, 90.

29. Nick Vujicic. http://www.lifewithoutlimbs.org, June 2008, 1.

30. Ibid.

31. M.G., D.D. Easton, *Easton's 1897 Bible Dictionary.* Tennessee: Thomas Nelson.

32. David Wilkerson. *Times Square Church Pulpit Series*, June 13, 2005.

33. ©1985 Cook Communications Ministries. *You Gotta Keep Dancin'* by Tim Hansel. Used with permission. May not be further reproduced. All rights reserved. 123.

Chapter Four

34. Author, Judson W. Van de Venter, 1855-1939, Composer, Winfield S. Weeden, 1847-1908.
35. Nancy Missler. *Private Worship: The Key to Joy.* Idaho: The King's High Way, 2002, 49.
36. Taken from *Amazing Grace, 366 Inspiring Hymn Stories for Daily Devotions* © Copyright 2002 by Kenneth W. Osbeck. Published by Kregel Publications, Grand Rapids, MI. Used by permission of the publisher. All rights reserved. 261.
37. Taken from *101 More Hymn Stories: The Inspiring True Stories Behind 101 Favorite Hymns* © Copyright 1985 by Kenneth W. Osbeck. Published by Kregel Publications, Grand Rapids, MI. Used by permission of the publisher. All rights reserved. 136.
38. Lisa Bevere, *Out of Control and Loving It!* (Lake Mary, FL, Charisma House, 2006), 63. used by Permission.
39. Swartz, 41.
40. Nancy Missler. "Faith in the Night Season, Remaining in His Presence," *Personal Update*, Koinonia House, October 2001.

Chapter Five

41. Three Dog Night, audiocassette. "One" Three Dog Night, MCA Records, 1969.
42. Reprinted from Shattered Dreams Copyright © 2001 by Lawrence J. Crabb Jr., PhD, PC. Waterbrook Press, Colorado Springs, CO. All rights reserved.
43. Chambers, January 29.
44. THE PROBLEM OF PAIN by C.S. Lewis copyright © C.S. Lewis Pte. Ltd. 1940.
45. Taken from *101 More Hymn Stories: The Inspiring True Stories Behind 101 Favorite Hymns* © Copyright 1982 by Kenneth W. Osbeck. Published by Kregel Publications, Grand Rapids, MI. Used by permission of the publisher. All rights reserved.183.

46. Nancy Missler. *The Choice*. Coeur d'Alene, Idaho: Koinonia House, 2001, 71.
47. Carolyn Custis James. *Lost Women of the Bible*: The *Women We Thought We Knew*. Grand Rapids, Michigan: Zondervan, 2008, 94.
48. Ibid.
49. Crabb, 94.

Chapter Six

50. *The American Heritage Dictionary of the English Language*, Fourth Edition. Massachusetts: Houghton Mifflin Harcourt, 2006, 991
51. "laugh." Merriam-Webster Online Dictionary. 2009.Merriam-Webster Online. 12 August 2009 <http://www.merriam-webster.com/dictionary/laugh>.
52. "Health Benefits of Humor and Laughter." July 2009 http://www.saladmaster.info/saladmaster50.html.
53. Excerpted with permission from "Humor, Laughter and Health: Bringing More Humor and Laughter into Our Lives." Visit http://www.helpguide.org/life/humor_laughter_health.htm to see the full article with links to related articles. © Helpguide.org. All rights reserved. This material is for information and support; not a substitute for professional advice.
54. ©1985 Cook Communications Ministries. *You Gotta Keep Dancin'* by Tim Hansel. Used with permission. May not be further reproduced. All rights reserved. 82.

Chapter Seven

55. Kathleen Prentice. "When a Caregiver Needs Care." *Heart Insight Magazine*. May 2008, http://www.heartinsight.com/pt/re/wkhc/fulltext.01271221-200802000-00009.htm;jsessionid=LXnhVvp RhGHbzKVsd2GyXsdZfyLsMKrnN8vTN1nWvTw2vTy7vLG L!-1179726830!181195629!8091!-1.
56. Tada, 133.
57. Jeff Kuntz. "Hey You!" E-mail to author. November 13, 2003.
58. W. Hodding Carter. "Heroes, Most Valuable Player." *Reader's Digest*, May 2008.

59. ©1985 Cook Communications Ministries. *You Gotta Keep Dancin'* by Tim Hansel. Used with permission. May not be further reproduced. All rights reserved. 66.
60. Charles Siebert. "Carol Palumbo Waits for Her Heart." *The New York Times Magazine*, April 13, 1997.

Chapter Eight

61. Steve Miller, "Fly Like an Eagle." The Steve Miller Band, Capitol, 1976.
62. "Bride dies during marriage's first dance." Used with permission of The Associated Press Copyright © 2009. All rights reserved. February 9.
63. Francois de Fenelon. *The Seeking Heart*, The SeedSowers Christian Publishing House, 1993. 115.
64. *The American Heritage Dictionary of the English Language, Fourth Edition.* Retrieved July 30, 2009, from Dictionary.com website: http://dictionary.reference.com/browse/stony.
65. Clara H. Scott ("Open My Eyes, That I May See") Richard Parrott, *Come Ye Apart* (now called *Reflections*) is a quarterly devotional published by the Nazarene Publishing House.

Conclusion

66. Swindoll, 148.
67. Ibid, 145.
68. Mike Webb. An e-mail to the author. February 2005.
69. Excerpted from the Revive Our Hearts radio broadcast, "When Thankfulness Seems Impossible" by Nancy Leigh DeMoss. www.reviveourhearts.com/radio/today/23187 November 26, 2002, March 2008.
70. David Wilkerson. "The Importance of Having the Peace of Christ." *Pulpit Series Newsletter*, November 13, 2006.

Glossary

71. *The American Heritage Dictionary of the English Language, Fourth Edition.* Retrieved July 30, 2009, from Dictionary.com website: http://dictionary.reference.com/browse/congenital.
72. "Depression." Medline Plus. US National Library of Medicine, July 31, 2009, http://www.nlm.nih.gov/medlineplus/depression.html.

CPSIA information can be obtained at www.ICGtesting.com
Printed in the USA
LVOW072355070212

267569LV00002B/1/P